A LOOK AT THE TOWN IN THE FIFTIES, SIXTIES AND SEVENTIES

CHORLEY REMEMBERED

A LOOK AT THE TOWN IN THE FIFTIES, SIXTIES AND SEVENTIES

CHORLEY REMEMBERED

JACK SMITH

First published in Great Britain byThe Breedon Books Publishing Company Limited
Breedon House, 44 Friar Gate, Derby, DE1 1DA. 1999

This paperback edition published in Great Britain in 2015 by DB Publishing, an imprint of
JMD Media Ltd

ISBN 978-1-78091-489-3

Printed and bound in the UK by Copytech (UK) Ltd Peterborough

CONTENTS

ACKNOWLEDGEMENTS

IN 1999, when I compiled the book *Chorley Through the 1950s*, I never thought that it would be followed in 2000, by a similar book covering the 1950s and 60s.

Both these books sold well, and feature a large number of Chorley people, many of whom I knew personally. And I am regularly stopped by strangers who say they, or their family or friends are in one of those books.

In the main, readers seems to have enjoyed leafing through the books. Finding a picture of a familiar face, or a location that they held special, has revived many treasured memories. There have been a few critics of course, particularly if a photograph of that critic is not shown on one of the pages.

When compiling these books, I am sometimes presented with a photograph along with a comment such as 'I don't know who it is, where it is, or when it is.' This means I can only approximate a date or location based on general historical knowledge and, inevitably, errors are sometimes made. But if a photograph is of interest, it seems a shame not to use it, even if little or nothing is known about it.

It has been gratifying to find that so much pleasure has been given to so many people who have read the two previous books. I have been told they have been sent to many parts of the world, where former Chorley people now live.

Places like Australia, New Zealand, USA, Canada, Brazil, Oman, Germany, France, Italy, and even on to an oil rig. It's nice to know that, in such places, a little bit of Chorley resides in book form at least. I was even told, by Chorley MP Lindsay Hoyle, who kindly attended a launch event in 2000, that he had deposited one of the books in the House of Commons library.

To have been able to compile yet another book in a similar vein is most rewarding. This time we look at the 1970s as well – a decade which many people may think is too recent to be written about. What do you think? Can you remember all the events of the 1970s?

Thank you to all who have obtained and read the two previous books. I only hope this third one will be enjoyed as much. My thanks to Chorley Central Library, and local Branch Libraries. To the *Chorley Guardian* newspaper, for permission to use many of the photographs which appeared in that paper from the 1950s to 70s. These had originally been purchased by readers, and kindly given or loaned to me. To Bob and Pat Catterall, Joan and Brian Ogden, Barrie and Teresa Holding, Jean and Keith Morris, John and Evelyn Smith, Ross and Chris Hubbold and Ken Gray.

Finally, to Miss Margaret Raby, former mayor of Chorley, Mrs Margaret Moorcroft, former mayoress and widow of former mayor, the late Jim Moorcroft, and to Mr Geoff Simons, another former mayor of Chorley. In addition, I would like to thank everyone else who has either loaned photographs or who has, in any other way, helped me in the production of the book. Thank you again.

Jack Smith
Chorley
Lancashire
September 2002.

INTRODUCTION

IN PREVIOUS books, I have discussed many aspects of Chorley life during the 1950s and yet, through examining further photographs of that decade, I find there are still so many more things to highlight and discuss. These are part of the town's social history, a history which tends to escape our notice, for it concerns everyday things. Things which can easily be lost if not recorded.

During the early part of 2002, I was described, in a local newspaper, as being 'The Time Unraveller', a term I quite liked, for it is true that I feel obscure and seemingly everyday occurrences should be recorded and explained. For posterity perhaps.

Sadly, we will not leave behind a record of concern for our countryside, as a legacy for future generations. Neither the environment nor remnants of our history have been well protected. Up to the 1950s, for example, it was said that 'from anywhere in Chorley, you could be in the open countryside in minutes'. That is something that can no longer be demonstrated.

The town of 2002 continues to spread outwards, with buildings covering mostly greenfield sites, especially in the Burgh Lane area, where it seems that the development will soon join Chorley with Coppull. Even Chorley Nab is under threat – the 'thin end of the wedge' – having been inserted into that area, with houses built (during the period covered by this book) on the site of the former Heapey bleach works.

Currently, the site of Talbot Mill is scheduled for redevelopment. At one time this complex was the biggest of its kind , not just in Britain, but in Europe. Yet a part of that mill could, surely, be retained and converted into useful accommodation. At least this would preserve some of the character of the area, and leave it as it was.

What of the Lower Healey works of T. Witter & Company? Is this site also to become a housing development? All of this is encroaching upon what is, perhaps, the one remaining icon in Chorley's countryside. An area which has been revered for many generations, where 'Nab Spout' water still runs as clear and as fresh in the 21st century, as it did for our grandparents. This place is 'Healey Nab', to give it its correct title, but it is better known as 'Chorley Nab'.

The recording of what seems, at the time, to be mundane happenings and events, a few years later takes on a nostalgic mantle. We comment how quaint something was, or how we never hear about something any more. Things tend to slip into obscurity. For instance, in the 1950s, the use of a 'cowrake' was commonplace, as were groups of children doing 'gailies', around an area. Everyday things in the 1950s, but not today.

New Roads

Today, there are so many new roads and housing developments in and around the town, as it increasingly sprawls outwards. Not only are street games no longer played as much as they were in the 1950s, but there are simply not the 'facilities' for those street games, even though 1950s facilities were, more often than not, the lamp posts, walls and pavements of every street cunningly adapted by ever-imaginative children.

Aside from this, the roads are so much busier today than they were in the 1950s – they are no longer safe places to play. Yet the proliferation of new roads remains in vogue at the beginning of the 21st century. New roads which, sadly, mean the increasing loss of fields and quiet walks that our parents knew so well and which we, as small children, recall ourselves.

Remember how the Wallets Wood walk used to be one of those special walks? It started in Tootell Street, by an old farm, in the days before the council house estate was built. After walking along a footpath where old railway sleepers stood on their ends, walkers emerged into open country – part of the former Gillibrand Estate. Then on through 'the Wallets', to enjoy water meadows and the meandering River Yarrow, with thick woodland on the right, covering the embankment to the river valley. Passing Chorley bleach works, and emerging at Common Bank Farm, perhaps even chatting with Mr and Mrs Harrison who were the occupants for many years. From here a choice – either to proceed to Charnock Richard over the river, or return home via Common Bank Lane and Southport Road. 'The Wallets Wood' walk was featured on many postcards of Chorley at one time, for it was once regarded as such a gem.

Who would have ever thought that this beautiful area would be completely devastated by the creation of part of the westerly bypass for the town? The construction has removed the wildlife, interrupted the peace and quiet, destroyed the scenery, the amenity, that was Wallets Wood. All of this was done so that more houses can be built in this former oasis – which will, of course, lead to even more cars on the streets.

But it does not stop there. The bypass now strives to cut through some of the woodland at Duxbury Estate as well, to emerge near the gate lodge to Duxbury Park on Bolton Road.

This is the legacy that we are leaving for future generations. It would seem that both our heritage, and the privileges our parents enjoyed – to have easy access to so much unspoilt countryside – have been 'cancelled'. What has been is no longer valued, and the priority often seems to be to build on as many green areas as possible – a self-feeding cycle of new roads and new houses.

Returning to those street games and those 'gailies' – why did we dress up when we had a 'gaily'? It seems that reason could become lost too, as could many other remnants of our town of 40 or 50 years ago, those we can see, and those we can remember.

Memories which, perhaps, can be etched by some outside event of national, or even worldwide importance. You will remember, no doubt, precisely what you were you doing when you heard that Elvis Presley or Marilyn Monroe had died, or when President Kennedy was shot.

It has been suggested to me, by several Chorley residents who have read my previous recollections of the town, that I should use some of these major events to help stimulate yet more memories of life in Chorley in the past. Some readers have also suggested that toys, games, household goods, etc, bought from local shops, will expand the memory still further. With this in mind, I have incorporated a few items of news from the years we will be looking at. I am also inserting a few advertisements for local shops, so you can look, once more, at the prices in pounds, shillings and pence. No doubt that will give the younger generations, and some of the older ones too, a different aspect to consider and, prompt a few questions too.

When Television Ruled

A well as discussing the toys we played with and the films we saw, I shall be looking at the television programmes we watched. What about those early shows of the 1950s? Now there is scope for some nostalgia. Do you actually recall when your parents first bought or rented a television set, or receiver as it used to be called, and how it took pride of place in the living room? And which shop did it come from? Remember those flickering, slightly fuzzy black and white images on 12ins screens? Remember how parents said to 'come and sit at the table', when you wanted to watch television? Or how you had to complete your homework before you could watch? Remember teatime, the whole family watching television together, especially on Saturday afternoons? It was certainly the first steps on the way to 'television meals' sitting on the settee. From the mid-1950s, we began to spend less time with friends and neighbours, as television-watching took over as the country's favourite leisure activity.

It's difficult to write a general introduction about the 1950s without referring to what it was like to live in the town. Somehow, in the 1950s, and even in the 60s, Chorley was rather like a big village – you knew so many of the people as you walked around the streets and the markets. Today, this is no longer true – hundreds of new houses have brought in many new people from outside of the town.

Although there was, undoubtedly, a village atmosphere to the town, Market Street was a major trunk road, which at weekends took all the traffic from Manchester and the Midlands to Southport, Blackpool and the Lake District. Combined with the extra traffic for the Saturday market, this made the town centre, and Market Street in particular, very busy. The narrow footpaths thronged with shoppers, who had their 'moans' about the difficulty of crossing the road, but accepted it as part of living in Chorley. It was a far cry from the main street of today – an almost 'clinical' street, the main bulk of the traffic having been diverted, and the street partially pedestrianised, though used for parking.

Although pedestrianisation is an essential part of today's living in a modern town, shops within those areas are a huge necessity as well. Yet many of the old shops have been swept away in the process of modernisation, many of them replaced by office blocks, which, it could be argued, should not really have preference in shopping areas at all. The centre of modern Chorley now has fewer shops than it had in the 1950s.

Market Days

But the markets remain, bringing the areas around, and in between, the covered market and the 'Flat Iron' markets, to life. However, there seem to be fewer stallholders selling 'special offers' from the back of big vans than there were in the 1950s.

Today's 'Flat Iron' has also been much reduced in size, as again the car has been given priority. In the 1950s, car parking on market days was permitted only for traders. Today a permanent public car park takes up half of the old 'Flat Iron', and even the remaining market area is now under the same threat. It is needed to replace parking spaces lost to the relocation of the bus station to land off Clifford Street. The bus station site is, itself, due for retail redevelopment.

For some 500 years Chorley has had a market charter, and is known around the county as a market town. An important part of the town's heritage, we must not lose any more of our market facility, if we are to still attract visitors. Perhaps helping to alleviate these fears is a proposal to re-establish a market in Market Street itself. Its name, of course, reflects the fact that within the last 300 years it was the site of a large market. This market could replace the 'Flat Iron'.

A street market, perhaps like the one at Skipton in Yorkshire, would certainly be an attraction, and one which might give the town a necessary tourism boost. At the very least it would ensure Chorley's 'market town' title would be retained.

Of course, we have to forfeit some things for improvements and modernisation to the townscape and its facilities. By and large these improvements are advantageous.

The footpaths of 1950s Market Street were quite narrow and tightly-packed with shoppers. Today we have wider footpaths and a more decorative street, with mosaic

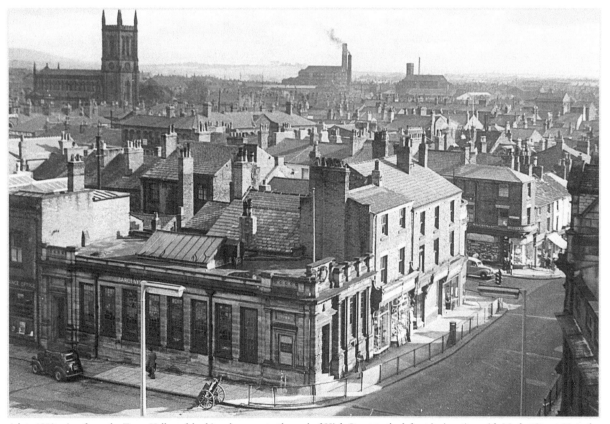

A late 1950s view from the Town Hall roof, looking down on to the end of High Street to the left, at its junction with Market Street. Note the former Barclays Bank building on the corner (with handcart outside).

tiles and street furniture, such as bollards and tall lamp standards, depicting images of the town and its river. The link with history remains, but there are certainly fewer people and many shops are empty.

Travellers, who were once directed through the main street, are now diverted along the town centre bypass lined with a new McDonalds and DIY stores. They no longer see the Chorley that they used to. That is reserved largely for those of us who live in and around the town. In view of the two bypasses constructed in the 1950s and 60s – the M6 and M61 motorways – the town centre bypass and the newer westerly bypass – it might be considered remarkable that there is any traffic in the town at all.

The proposed developments are for the future but, it has often been said, we must look to the past to predict the future. We have seen the 'Flat Iron' nibbled away over the years, piece by piece for a variety of developments. Firstly a swimming baths, a parking area, and then an extension to the baths. Next for a refreshment bar, a squash court and a gas showroom. Finally, another chunk was taken for yet another car park, and today's 'Flat Iron' market is about one-third the size it used to be, and it now seems an inevitability that we will lose it altogether.

Bath Night

The swimming baths bring back wonderful memories for so many of us. They were so much a part of life. We all recall the main pool, and those cold seats arranged around it, as well as the changing rooms of course, but how many of us recall another familiar feature – one which provided for those of us without 'plumbed-in' baths?

In the 1950s there were still plenty of houses which did not have a hot water system, except for a gas geyser in the kitchen. The old tin bath was still used in many houses around Chorley, and often that hot water came from the tank incorporated in the living room 'Lancashire Range'.

Of course, some of us were lucky enough to have relatives with bathrooms with modern facilities, but by and large these were in the minority. and asking whether you could go round to their house for a bath on a particular night could prove embarrassing. There were just two alternatives – the tin bath or Chorley baths.

Here, there was a facility known as 'slipper baths'. These were just normal baths, each in an individual panelled cubicle room. You could pay to hire towels and soap, or simply bring your own. Many will remember sitting in the bath but keeping an eye on the top of the 8ft-high panels in case a head popped over them.

Much of the embarrassment the 'slipper baths' probably came from a feeling of self-consciousness about having to use the facility. There were, of course, separate bathing facilities for men and women. The facility was well used in the 1950s. I am uncertain when these were closed, but it could have been in the 1960s.

Going to the Pictures

What of entertainment in those days? In the 1950s Chorley people had five cinemas to choose from – the Plaza, the Royal, the Odeon, the Empire and the Pavilion – some even changing their programme halfway through the week. This multi-choice was great, but if there were several good pictures on in the same week, you not usually afford to see them all.

It was not unusual to go to the pictures three or four times a week . Admission prices might vary from one shilling to almost three shillings (5p to 15p today). In the 1950s, even such an apparently small amount as this represented a significant investment – at least to those of us who were children.

Consider the wages of the time in this context. As an apprentice in the early 1950s, I was earning around £3 a week for five days' work. Even skilled men were getting less than £20. So it was with some trepidation that you asked your parents for a little more money towards the end of the week.

Sadly, towards the end of the 1950s the cinema's popularity dwindled with the advent of television. When films began to appear regularly on television, particularly those of favourites like Laurel and Hardy, the Three Stooges or George Formby, there was little need to pay to go to the pictures to see them.

The 1960s saw an even sharper decline in cinema audiences. During this decade we saw three of our locals – the Royal, the Empire and the Pavilion – close. The latter had a revival in the 1970s when it reopened for a few months, before closing again. Plans for conversion to a dance hall, with a cabaret, and a smaller cinema complex, was mooted, but came to nothing.

By the 1970s we had two cinemas only, the Odeon and the Plaza, both of which at one time were regarded as

In the middle of Market Street now, standing at the bottom of St George's Street, and looking to the west side of the street. Here – so typical of the time – it was virtually impossible to cross the road due to heavy traffic. The Royal cinema is visible in the centre of this photograph, taken mid-1950s.

shows on Sunday night, when radio artistes and bands came to play live on stage.

Once more we were reduced to one cinema with two screens, which now carried the name of Studio Two, not the Plaza. This loss of old established names seems to have become common in the area, even in the late 20th century and into the 21st, especially where pub names are concerned. But more on that later in the illustrated chapters.

Chorley has been without a cinema now for over 30 years – – yet three of those cinema buildings are still standing at the time of writing – the former Odeon, Plaza and Empire. More recently there has been an upsurge in cinema audiences, as people become discontented with television and look to the modern, luxurious and exciting new multi-screen cinemas springing up in many of the towns surrounding Chorley. These multiplexes are regularly attended by a large numbers of local people. Is there a place for such a complex in Chorley nowadays? I would think so.

Chorley's 'posh' picture places – those you went to on a Saturday night. Incidentally, did you know that the Plaza was originally proposed to be called the Coronation, because it was built during the coronation year of King George VI and Queen Elizabeth (the late Queen Mother) in 1937?

In January 1971, the Plaza closed temporarily with promises of conversion work, although locals feared that it would, like so many cinemas across the country at that time, never reopen. But at the end of the month the Plaza did reopen, now converted to a two-screen cinema.

For a short time Chorley cinemagoers could choose from three films in two locations. But in February 1971, the Odeon closed for good. This was something of a sad event, for it had been considered Chorley's premier cinema. The Plaza had been more regarded for its stage

Dancing the Night Away

We danced a lot in the 1950s and 60s, didn't we? The local newspapers carried so many advertisements for dance halls of all kinds and we were never stuck for a place to go dancing, either in the town or outside of it. These venues catered for young and old, with 'old time', 'modern ballroom' and the type preferred by younger people, which played the music young people liked and which, as yet, had no specific name, but for 'jive' or 'bop'. The term discotheque had not yet come into being.

Many of us remember the times when we were allowed to dance our 'modern' way (to jive that is), in the corners of the main dance floor, only to get frowned at by the older set. Now we have become the elders ourselves and wonder just where have all the dance venues, the ones we knew so well, gone.

Consider all the places we could go, yet these too were in decline by the end of the 1960s. Was it that many of them were acoustically unsuitable, like the Town Hall used to be? Though I doubt if we really considered that. Once again the blame was laid on the advent of television, causing more people to stay indoors rather than frequent the dance halls.

It's funny how the places we danced at in the 1950s and 60s had a sort of 'class' about them. The civic dances were all held in the Royal Oak, which was the town's top venue – always bow-ties and evening dresses at these occasions.

The few dances that were held in the Town Hall's Assembly Room, as it was then called, were usually held by clubs and other organisations. The first private club to use the Assembly Room for a dance in the post-war years was St George's Institute, on 16 January 1953. The existing restrictions for the use of the room were lifted to allow a total of 400 people to attend the function.

Other dance halls catered for the rest of the town. Which one you went to depended on which age group you were in. There was, of course, the Tudor and some of the church halls, such as St Mary's on Devonshire Road. Then there was the 'Vic', which was also a place where many went to learn ballroom dancing, tutored by Mr and Mrs Entwistle. There were other places as well, such as the Ambulance Hall, and the Co-op Hall in Little Steeley Lane.

How about all the places we visited for a night out, from time to time, outside of town, travelling by bus to Bolton Palais, Rivington Barn or the Highways Hostel in Euxton? Perhaps the premier out-of-town venue, though, was Blackpool on a Saturday night which we reached by train. Many readers will remember them as rather special trips.

Archaeological Society

The 1950s was also a time when a new society was launched in Chorley – the Archaeological Society which was established in 1953. The society followed their initial meetings with an exhibition in Astley Hall, relating to the pre-history of Chorley and district. This exhibition created a lot of attention, for many of the exhibits were on display for the first time. Items such as prehistoric flint tools found on the local moors, and Roman pottery

discovered at the Walton-le-Dale Roman site were displayed. I was one of the founder members of the Archaeological Society in Chorley.

A Mill Town

There were a great many people working in the cotton mills of Chorley in the 1950s, but do you recall the incident which happened in February 1952 at Smethursts' North Street Mill? It happened on a Friday afternoon, when the machines were shut down rather too quickly. This caused the 25ft-diameter flywheel, which was driving the spinning machinery in the mill, to increase in speed. The engine that was driving the flywheel also speeded up, and the speed restricting governor failed to shut off the steam. This caused the flywheel to disintegrate whilst rotating at great speed, destroying the engine house and adjoining buildings, plus sending pieces of iron through the air to land on houses. One person was killed and others were injured in this incident.

As we have just said, the many cotton mills in Chorley were employers of a great many local people in the 1950s and 60s, although between 1950 and 1962 no less than 12 local mills had closed. Many of them were subsequently demolished. Since that time I have been trying to record the passing of the cotton industry locally, for this is another area which has had little historical coverage to date.

When 'cotton ruled' in Chorley, the town seemed almost empty during the July holiday period, when all the mills closed down. There was an overall quiet about the town, somehow, for with the mills closed down, the works' buzzers, which were so much a part of daily life in a cotton town, were no longer heard. They sounded at the start of shift in the morning, and at the end of the working day. Many works or mills had different starting and finishing times and when you heard each of them, you could keep track of the time.

The demise of Chorley's cotton trade not only affected the spinning and weaving mills, but also those which were concerned with the finishing of the woven cloth, the bleaching and dyeing works. Many of these had to lay-off employees or introduce short-time working.

By the 1970s, most of the remaining empty mills had been converted into smaller units or had been demolished. There were only two manufacturers of yarn or woven material left – Talbot Spinning and Weaving

A view looking north from the new Crosse Hall Bridge with the new Froom Street Bridge in the mid-distance, finished and in use. To the right, the road up to the 'Nab Quarry'. Talbot Mill, to the left of centre, viewed in 1968 during building of the M61.

Company, and Messrs J.D. Lawrence & Co Ltd, at Lyons Lane Mills. Even these firms had adapted to use man-made as well as natural fibres in their operations.

Talbot Mill ceased its spinning operations in their five-storey mill in the later months of 1991. By the end of the year, all machinery had been removed. Demolition of the spinning mill began in February 1992, and continued until April, by which time the site had been levelled. The weaving section of the mill continued working under Courtaulds Ltd, where items such as cotton cabinet towels and woven polyester sacks were manufactured. In 2000 all the weaving operations were stopped.

Between late 2000 and late 2001, all reusable machinery had been removed, and the deserted mill vandalised – some 90 per cent of its roof slates had been stolen. It is hard to imagine that this fine mill – once the biggest in Europe – had been reduced to a vandalised shell in just one year. Messrs Lawrence, off Lyons Lane,

continues to produce fine spun yarns and woven materials, although now using man-made fibres and the most up-to-date machinery, with looms running at over 600 picks per minute, compared with the old Lancashire looms which worked at about 150 picks. During early 2002, I was privileged to tour this mill and was sad to think that this is the last working mill in Chorley, hence my concern and interest in recording it while still working. The end of an era is certainly in sight. In the early 1950s, some 25 mills in and around Chorley were busy in the cotton trade, employing over 4,000 workers. By the end of the 1970s, that figure was reduced to only 700. Today less than 200 are in the employ of spinning and weaving.

Some 70s Optimism

Perhaps the 1970s offered some optimism when, despite the demise of cotton manufacture, other small industries were established in the area. Also, the Royal Ordnance Factory (ROF) was still employing a large workforce. But even there, the workforce had been gradually declining. In the 1950s, when many new workers had been taken on due to the government's re-arming policy some 4,000 people were employed there. That figure had shrunk to 1,600 in the 1970s, and was still declining.

It might be argued that we allowed our textile industry to disappear by 'stealth'. The trade suffered so badly when we allowed overseas companies access to our expert technology and techniques. Not only were these companies able to sell back to us cheaper finished products, allowing buyers to bypass our home produced goods entirely, but they also began to produce the textile machinery much cheaper than we could either in Lancashire, or Britain as a whole. This surely added insult to injury.

All of this happened despite the warnings coming out of Lancashire from cotton producers who so clearly saw the writing on the wall. There were protests from textile workers, and the lobbying of MPs to stop the importation of cottons from abroad. All these actions had no effect, and, ultimately, this led to the demise of the cotton trade in Lancashire as a whole. Who was it who said in the House of Commons that 'Britain's Bread hangs by Lancashire's Thread'?

Railway Decline

Just like the decline and closure of the mills in and around Chorley, the enormous changes that have taken place on our local railways, in the period covered by these pages, could hardly have been envisaged. Back in the 1950s, it seemed as though things would never change.

The railway held a special place in all our hearts. The train was used regularly for local journeys, although not often for great distances. That was reserved for holiday times.

Along with many other lads, I was more interested in the steam locomotives that pulled the trains. We were 'spotters', and proud of it. In those days, there was no derogatory term, like 'anoraks', used. The 'spotter' fraternity greatly anticipated trips by train, particularly those that took us outside our own region.

There was, of course, one British Rail network, but these were divided into regions derived from the pre-nationalisation networks prior to 1948. These regions were: our own Midland Region, ex-LMS; the Eastern Region, ex-LNER; the Western Region, ex-GWR; and the Southern Region, ex-Southern Railway. Visits to these other regions meant seeing different locomotives, thus travelling by rail was more than just a journey for those of us who were 'spotters' in the 1950s. It was an adventure into foreign territory.

We could catch the train from Chorley direct to Wigan, travelling over what was locally called the White Bear Line, taken from the name of the station at Lower Adlington. This line diverted from the main Chorley to Bolton line, less than a half mile before the present Adlington station.

Blackburn was another main town we could reach directly. At Chorley station, there was a bay platform, where trains to Blackburn and/or Wigan were parked at times. There were, of course, the normal 'through' trains between Blackburn and Wigan, but the bay trains were purely local. One of these which achieved fame in earlier years was one nicknamed 'Chorley Bob'.

The railway line to Blackburn was soon climbing, the engine working hard from Stump Lane Bridge up the hill to Withnell station (Abbey Village). The train passed over the Botany Viaduct (demolished in the late 1960s), stopping at Heapey, Brinscall, Withnell, Feniscowles, Cherry Tree, then Blackburn.

Of all the stations on this well-used local line, Heapey was one which achieved greatest popularity with dedicated hikers and casual walkers. The walkers would either wander from Chorley to White Coppice for a day's picnic, then catch the train back to Chorley, or vice versa. The hikers would start, perhaps, from Blackburn and walk via Tockholes and Great Hill through White Coppice, and return to Blackburn by train. Aptly the nickname given to this line was the 'Hikers' Line'.

It was also possible to travel direct to Horwich station by train. These trains, too, used Chorley station's short three-coach bay platform, which was on the Preston side platform. The trains had to cross over to the Manchester line when they set off towards Horwich or Wigan.

The station at the Royal Ordnance Factory, the 'ROF Halt', was in use until the mid-1960s, when buses replaced the trains. There were several small 'mineral' or branch lines in and around Chorley. From Heapey station there was a line to Heapey bleach works, which was used to take coal and other raw materials into the works, and bring finished goods out. They had their own steam locomotive as well.

The Dacca works on Water Street had its own internal rail system, with sidings and its own locomotive. The collieries at Welsh Whittle had a line running from near to Coppull Mill, north of the station, across the fields and A49 road to the colliery.

Another colliery railway came off the main line to the south of Coppull station, to run over the A49 road also, to Chisnall Hall Colliery. Ellerbeck Colliery was served by a branch line that came off the Chorley to Adlington line, close to Rawlinson Lane Bridge, crossing the canal, going under Rawlinson Lane and over Wigan Lane to the colliery site.

From the early 1960s though, following the drastic 'Beeching Cuts', we saw the Blackburn to Wigan line run down, and in 1967 it was closed. The stations at Coppull, White Bear and Balshaw Lane all closed.

Almost 40 years later, Balshaw Lane station has been rebuilt, and rumours that Coppull station may also be reopened come and go. The former ROF Halt remains standing, although no longer in the middle of the Royal Ordnance Factory, three-quarters of that factory having been demolished.

The station will soon serve a new village being created on the site of the factory, to be called Buckshaw Village. I wonder if the station will be renamed 'Buckshaw Halt' when it is reopened?

Through the 1950s we were still able to walk alongside the railway goods warehouse that backed on to Railway Street, which fronted to the goods yard itself. From here, in the early part of the decade, horses still hauled goods to places around the town, to be eventually superseded by the little three-wheel vehicles called Scamell Scarabs.

A rail line crossed over Railway Street, near its junction with Lyons Lane. This line used to lead to the Chorley Railway Wagon Works. The road entrances to this works were Albion Street, off Bolton Street, and Whittle Street, off Lyons Lane, immediately next to the pub called Castle Inn. That stood at the Railway Street/Lyons Lane corner.

Off Clifford Street was Brunswick Street with its low railway bridge, often the scene of tall vehicle 'decapitations'. To the left is Chorley railway station, with a train in the platform. To the right is the former coal yard, with dealers' sheds visible over the wall. Photograph *c.*1971

The goods warehouse was demolished in the 1960s, along with the large sheds off Clifford Street that belonged to Messrs Haydock & Co. The old stone warehouse adjoining the pedestrian subway at the railway station was also demolished at this time. Messrs Thomas Witter's Lightweight Linoleum Products, a company which had relied heavily upon the goods yard, still despatched their goods from Chorley, a new shed having been built near the front of Chorley Station. This was latterly used by Messrs Stewart Longton Caravans until their relocation to the former Friday Street coal yard site.

The Friday Street coal yard and sidings extended from Brunswick Street to Stump Lane Bridge. In the 1950s, it was a busy site, where rows of coal wagons, often bearing the names of the colliery they came from, were unloaded either on to stacks, or into sacks then weighed, and loaded on to local delivery wagons. All the coal merchants had little offices behind the Brunswick Street wall where Chorley residents called in to pay bills or order a delivery of coal.

One of the factors which speeded the decline of the yard was, of course, the 'clean air policy' and 'smokeless zone' delineation of the 1960s. There was great fear of more 'smog' areas. Remember how that word, 'smog', came into being? When it was revealed that the awful hazard was a mixture of coal *sm*oke, and *fo*g,? The introduction of 'smokeless fuels' and the increase in houses using central heating also contributed to the gradual decline. By the 1970s, the coal yard was host to only one or two coal wagons, and the merchants' offices were mostly empty.

The Blackburn to Wigan railway was in operation until 1967, when the tracks were lifted. For a time, a short length of track ran alongside the coal yard and under Stump Lane Bridge, almost as far as Rylands Crossing Bridge, which was used to store rail vehicles for a time, and to allow shunting alongside Mayfield Mill into the coal yard or the old warehouse off Stump Lane, which still stands today.

Highways and Byways

What of the roads and streets of Chorley? How did they change from the 50s to 70s, and how do they compare with today? Just where does one start? Let's begin with our main street. Part of the A6 'trunk route', which formed the main north-south passage through Chorley, it was the busiest road in the town. Wagons travelling between Scotland and the southern counties of England were once a familiar sight. From the north the route ran along Preston Road, Park Road, Market Street, Bolton Street and Bolton Road, in the direction of Manchester. This route had been in place since 1822, when Park Road was built in the form of a high embankment across the valley of the River Chor. The older route, dating from the 17th century, ran along what later became Preston Road, Preston Street, Water Street, Church Brow, Market Street and Bolton Street.

The coming of the day-trip era – when wagonettes, and later the early charabancs, took parties to the seaside towns along the Lancashire coast – saw an increase in motor traffic the routes serving those destinations. Southport is less than 20 miles from Chorley; Blackpool about 30 miles. Morecambe and the Lake District, part of which was in Lancashire, were popular destinations for the early 'charas', and later the motor coaches. As well as local traffic, coaches from Manchester and the Midlands queued through Bolton Street and Market Street, en route to the resorts. Car ownership levels rose during the 1950s, adding yet more traffic to the roads. It was difficult to get across the main street. And there were no 'Belisha' crossings yet. It was essential that one, two or even three policemen would be on point duty, to stop the traffic periodically to allow pedestrians to cross the street.

By the early 1960s, the volume of traffic had reached a point when urgent action had to be taken. Traffic lights were erected at Skew Bridge, Heath Charnock, where the A6 route turns off the Bolton Road, and those traffic lights at Bolton Street/ Lyons Lane crossroads, which had been 'on trial' since 1958, were made 'official' and became permanent.

Despite the assurances of the local authority that traffic through Chorley had decreased since the opening of the Preston Bypass (which was later to become the M6 motorway) in 1958, this was certainly not visible by the traffic flow through the town. If anything traffic appeared to have increased, because the attraction of driving along this new 'motor road' at high speed was drawing visitors from as far away as the Midlands.

It was only in 1963 that the section of road which passed to the west of Chorley was completed. This was the Bamber Bridge to Lymm section. We had been told that Chorley would soon have its own bypass, and that it

Market Street ends at the junction with Pall Mall and Bolton Street. In *c*.1973, a mini roundabout was being created to help traffic flow at this three-way junction.

would be a motorway route at that. Yet when the so-called Chorley bypass opened in 1963, passing just two miles west of the town, none of the roads out of Chorley had direct access to the new route.

All street lighting in Chorley was by gas until the early 1950s, when we saw the first electric street lighting. Were any readers in Market Street that night when those first electric lights were switched on in the early 1950s? I was there, and, like everyone else, marvelled at this modern lighting.

However, in some parts of town, the streets and alleyways were almost Dickensian by contrast, many of them still gas-lit into the 1960s. This was especially so in those streets which had older property, much of which would be demolished in later years. Similarly, although the main streets of Chorley had been resurfaced with tarmacadam, many of the other streets still retained their

cobbles, even until the 1970s. Even today we can see, through holes in the tarmac, that those cobbles are still there, just below the surface. We had a number of unadopted streets in the 1950s and 60s, but either these are a long-abandoned practice, or the signs have now been removed.

Modern Chorley has, perhaps, twice as many streets as it did in the 1950s due to the large number of houses built since that time. So much so that it's a bit of an embarrassment when we are often stopped by someone, who asks about a particular road in the town, only for us never to have heard of it. How many of us know the names of the roads, closes and drives in these new housing developments are called? Not many of us, I'm sure.

Building continues, and most of it on what were once rural sites, destroying ever-increasing amounts of our local countryside. Take, for example, the hundreds of houses built where there used to be a Burgh Lane. Or how Astley Village now sprawls between Southport Road and Euxton Lane, and continues to grow. There is little redevelopment of brown field sites, where previously old houses or industrial premises once stood. The one exception to this is the former ROF site.

The 1970s was a time when the increase in cars saw Chorley streets becoming choked with parked cars. Here again voices were raised for the local authority to take action. The problem was precisely what action to take. There were just not sufficient places to allow parking off the streets. One major scheme that was suggested caused some lengthy discussion.

It was suggested that a road, built on 'stilts' be constructed across Water Street and Chorley 'bottoms'. It would come off Park Road near the former Parish Institute, and be carried over to join with Bengal Street at the corner of Hollinshead Street. Beneath this road, was to be a multi-storey car park.

The road scheme proposal didn't last very long, but the multi-storey car park was seriously considered for quite a while. In retrospect, this might have been a sensible idea. It was to be built on the former gasworks site and would not have stood above the normal street level, the multistoreys being underground. The site was eventually used for more housing.

Our 'Lost' Buildings

During the period we are looking at in this volume, many of the well-known buildings in and around the town were demolished. Many, by now, will have been forgotten. A later chapter of the book looks at many of them, and that, no doubt, will evoke some memories. Many of the 'lost' buildings were domestic properties – a typical part of the townscape we knew so well. But they had become unfit to live in, and thus were demolished.

They had character, and many of them were built from stone. Unfortunately, the cost to repair and modernise them was not justified. It was cheaper to demolish and rebuild. The 1950s and 60s saw many of the town's council estates being built, following on from the post-war years and temporary housing (the 'prefabs') that had been built in several locations. However, the late 1940s had seen some permanent council houses built like those in the Springs Road, The Crescent and Harrison Road areas.

But it was not just middle and working-class domestic property that we lost. Some of our old halls, which featured prominently in important periods of Chorley's history were also demolished. One such was Duxbury Hall, the home of a branch of the Standish family, and a place which could have been one of Chorley's greatest tourist attractions. It had connections with the legendary Myles Standish, who sailed to America on the *Mayflower*, hired by the Pilgrim Fathers for his military expertise.

This famous figure in history helped found the first colony there, and became a leading figure within the community. As to whether or not he was born at Duxbury is uncertain, and volumes of theories about his ancestry have been written in the past. But, whether or not he was born here is not of vital importance. Evidence suggest that he knew Duxbury. It may well have been one of his favourite places, and one he often visited, perhaps in childhood. Local lore suggests that Myles Standish worshipped at Chorley Parish Church, in the Standish family pew. Perhaps more encouraging still is the location of the pilgrim's death in 1656. When the *Mayflower* pilgrims dissolved their communal farm, each settler was granted a certain parcel of land, Standish received a sizable area which he named 'Duxbury' – surely an indication of his Chorley heritage?

There is, of course, the doubtful baptism record of Myles in Chorley Parish Church registers. If this is genuine, and we know that the Standishes of Duxbury attended the Parish Church, why was Myles baptised there if he was not born at Duxbury? From a historian's point of view, I am happy to know that the facts suggest that he had a great affinity with Duxbury.

The Americans at Washington Hall, in Chorley, during World War Two, revelled in the premise that they were encamped close to the birthplace of such a famous person. In 1942 their Independence Day church service was held at Chorley Parish Church, and the 'Stars and Stripes' was presented to the church, to hang over the Standish family pew. Many of the officers and men from Washington Hall also visited Duxbury Hall privately, between 1942 and 1945.

Unbelievably, Duxbury Hall – a place associated with a family, one of whom was a founding father of America – was demolished in 1952. There was surely huge potential for developing the site into a major tourist attraction, but this was not even considered in the 1950s. This was strange, because Duxbury Park had held

Of our local halls, the list has been halved from what it used to be. So much for the protection of our heritage! One such hall was this at Duxbury. It was demolished in 1952, following years of neglect, which allowed the internal down spouts to leak and the beam ends to rot.

tercentenary celebrations for Myles Standish and this had attracted many visitors from the USA.

Clayton Hall was another of the casualties of the period. This hall, latterly a farm, had 16th-century origins with subsequent rebuilds. It was surrounded by a moat and had belonged to an important local family. Though a listed building, which should have protected the hall, it suffered the indignation of being 'vandalised' by a Leyland company who owned it. Stone lintels, door jambs, stone window frames and roofing tiles were removed. Clayton Hall stood alongside a public footpath and, although a notice had allegedly been served on the owners to repair the damage, they had caused, this was not done. This enforcement notice does not seem to have been implemented, and the building was allowed to fall prey to more 'vandalism'. It became so dangerous that it was demolished in the 1970s.

Interestingly, during 2000, I was involved in the compilation of a report for the Commission for New Towns in Lancashire, to carry out an archaeological/historical survey of the site and immediate area. This was with a view to carrying out some restoration work at the hall , which might include creating a consolidated ruin, to show what the hall used to be like, as well as making the site more attractive, with information boards regarding its history.

At the time of writing these pages, in April 2002, work at the Clayton Hall site is being carried out, and the walls of the hall are now visible, after being covered with a pile of rubble since the 1970s. It's gratifying to know that one's input into such a project is finally producing an end result. At least there will be something for future generations to see at this historical site.

Clayton Hall was not the last to be demolished in the area. In 1967, Bagganley Hall, off Eaves Lane in Chorley met the same fate. It was a 17th-century building, which may have been built on the site of an earlier hall. The house could well have been associated with the Royal

Forest of Healey, and the 'parkers' who looked after the forest for the local lords – in this case the Barons of Manchester, who hunted Healey and Horwich Chase.

The hall was demolished because it was in the way of the proposed M61 motorway route. In fact, the house and farm buildings adjoining lay in the way of the northbound carriageway, hard shoulder and verge. It did not block the whole of the proposed route. One cannot but help asking the question as to why the motorway route could not have been deviated slightly, to miss the hall building at least, so that it need not have been demolished. Other 'lost' buildings will be discussed in the chapter 'Some Buildings Recalled'. Perhaps the chapter will also remind readers of those buildings I do not have space to show.

So Many Changes

To summarise, many of the changes which have taken place in Chorley from the 1950s to the 1970s can, by and large, be attributed to the effects of the motor car.

The 1950s was also a time when the need for new schools became urgent , both for primary and secondary education , which was a new concept. The mid-1950s saw a sudden rise in school-age children, the result of a post-war increase in birthrate. It was a matter of national concern, and was given the nickname of 'the Bulge'. In Chorley the problem led to the building of St Alban's School and Southlands. The lack of local school accommodation was first highlighted at the former Union Street Grammar School where, at the end of the 1950s, classes were being held in cloakrooms and corridors.

This led to the building of a new grammar school in Southport Road, which was completed by December 1960, although the school would not be in full operation until 1962. After the old school premises were closed, they were taken over by Chorley College of Education, a teacher-training college.

The early to mid-1960s saw the need for yet more schools and houses. The local authority's estates at Highfield, Tootell Street, Thorn Hill and Liptrott were all built around this time, expanding the suburban area, yet few changes had taken place on the main streets.

The traffic was still heavy despite the opening of that M6 motorway, which the Minister of Transport had mooted as a 'bypass' for Chorley. Three years after its completion, in 1965, Chorley had its longest recorded queue of traffic, which extended from the Town Hall, where traffic turned to go to Southport, southwards past Wigan Lane corner with Bolton Road, and almost to the 'Skew Bridge' in Heath Charnock.

In the late 1960s, it was announced that the proposed new town for Central Lancashire would indeed get the go-ahead. It would be based around the towns of Chorley, Leyland and Preston. The scheme had been around for some years, and fears that the area would become an overspill for Manchester people meant that it was not greeted with much enthusiasm.

Throughout the 1960s Chorley town centre saw numerous changes. The last court was held in the old police station in St Thomas's Road in March 1965 – the same month that the station was relocated to its temporary home at Woodlands Hostel.

The designs for the new police station appeared in local newspapers and the Chorley public complained that its proposed location, next to the Victorian Town Hall, was unsuitable, given its design. It was suggested, in unofficial circles, that the new building should be erected at the Woodlands site. The reasoning for this was that the architecture of the new station would 'balance' with the new Grammar School at the other side of the road in Southport Road. However most of the work on the new police station was completed by 1967, though some internal work was still to be done.

In 1965 it was announced that a new motor road would be built between Manchester and Preston, which would interchange with other new motorways, and extend into Yorkshire. This new road would apparently pass through Chorley, relieving any existing through-traffic problems, effectively becoming a bypass for the town. Once again we were officially being promised another bypass. The Nine Arch Viaduct at Botany was demolished in 1968 to allow work on the new road, which we had learned was to be called the M61.

The Chorley section of the M61, between Anderton and Bamber Bridge, was opened in 1969. That same year, Haydocks timber merchants closed in Clifford Street. The building remained empty for a time, and it seemed it would be demolished. It did survive, however, and was converted into a supermarket in two phases, which saw completion in 1970.

The 1970s would still see traffic problems in the centre of Chorley, but rather than through-traffic causing

This overview of Botany was taken from the top of the railway viaduct during preparation for demolition. The old canal bridge is at middle left. Talbot Mill is in the distance to the right. The M61 is being created to the right, where the machines are working in October 1968.

problems, this time it was street parking. The decade also saw environmental and conservation awareness raised, with various schemes suggested, and groups becoming involved with local projects. It also saw royal visitors such as the Queen, Prince Philip and Princess Margaret.

Yet, more than anything else, it was probably the building of the new town under the Central Lancashire Development Corporation that preoccupied the local media.

Compulsory purchase orders became commonplace, and we wondered what the future would hold for us once we were living within a new town.

THE 1950S

THIS is the third book I have compiled in which I recall the 1950s. The first covered the 1950s only, the second the 1950s and 60s, and in this volume I attempt to cover three decades: the 1950s, 60s and the 70s.

For me, the 50s, was a time of 'growing up', of leaving school, of learning an apprenticeship at Horwich Locomotive Works – a time when steam locomotives still held sway on our railways – of completing that apprenticeship, and joining a shipping company – The Peninsular & Oriental Steam Navigation Company (P&OSN Co) – which had a fleet of ships sailing out of London to the Far East and Australia, calling at most of the major ports en route.

It was a decade when that so-called 'learning curve', of which we hear so much, proved to be much bigger than I anticipated. Not only from an educational point of view, with day school and night school at Horwich Tech, and learning the skills of a trade at the works, but further afield too. Armed with what I thought was plenty of experience and technical knowledge, I joined my first ship at King George Dock in London's East End.

As it happened, the first ship on which I worked was regarded as 'not very big'. It was around 18,000 tons, and a passenger ship, which sailed to the Far East several times a year. When joining a shipping company as an engineer, you spent a few months learning about boilers and engines on ships still in port, gaining a general idea of how the whole system of engines, and a ship's 'hotel' facilities – passenger accommodation etc, worked. You were ready to go to sea only when you could prove you had sufficient working knowledge about all the systems, and could pass a written examination plus a question and answer test. But my confidence was knocked sideways when I began working in the engine room of a twin-screw turbine ship. There were pipes everywhere: above, below and on every side. Everything was duplicated and cross-connected. There were three types of water being used, which had to be kept separate, and all the steam drains ran into a common source, so the condensed steam could be reused. That was just the basics.

What, you might say, has this anecdote got to do with Chorley? Well, the point I try to make is how, in time, you become familiar with new or changed environments. How, by recording what you see or hear, by familiarity and experience, you learn what is happening around you.

I had had a good grounding on how to record what was happening around me after I became interested in Chorley's history and archaeology, for I had been making notes about the town for some years – even during the time I was serving an apprenticeship. I had a good tutor in the form of the late Alderman Charlie Williams JP, a friend of my father's, who was a devoted local historian. It was he who imparted to me the importance of recording – not just about the prehistoric, Roman or later periods, but about the social events going on in Chorley at that time, the 1950s.

Between 1949 and 1953, I accompanied my mentor around the town which he knew so well, a town where he had been a postman for 30 years. Much of that time he had spent on delivery rounds in Chorley, Heapey and the Wheelton area. Mr Williams lived in Queens Road, quite close to my own home. It was from this area that we made our forays into Chorley, to look at some of the old property that was still present in the town in the first few years of the 1950s.

Living close to the park, it was natural that we visited Astley Hall. Here in the early 1950s, restoration work was going on in the courtyard and, as Mr Williams knew the hall curator – who was also its librarian, Mr Blackburn – we had access to places which were closed to the general public. I was intrigued with the timber structure. Much of it was in poor condition. It was essential that the work was done to prevent further decay.

Astley Hall was one of the first places I ever visited with a historian of note, and where I met with a curator. That was in 1951. I could never have imagined in my wildest dreams that, about 25 years later, I would be the founding chairman of the Astley Hall Society, and involved with the opening of the courtyard to the public for the first time .

Mr Williams and I visited Chorley Parish Church, to view it from a historical perspective. This was most revealing, for it was the church I attended regularly at that time, and I was a chorister and bell-ringer. But to see the church from a historian's point of view brought the textbooks to life.

About 1953, many of the old buildings dating from the mid-19th century were still occupied. I noted in one journal how we visited what used to be handloom weavers' cottages in Parker Street and off Bolton Street, in King Street. I suppose this was the time when I became interested in industrial history.In both these locations we went into the houses and saw the actual cellars where looms had been 100 years before. All the cottages had steps from the footpath up to the living room, which allowed a window to be built at ground level, to allow light to enter the cellar.

Although we did not enter every former handloom weavers' cottage we saw, we visited their locations. They were concentrated around the 'Big Lamp' and Bolton Street areas.They were located in King Street, Queen Street West, Bolton Street, Standish Street, Albion Street, Fleet Street, Moor Street and Anderton Street, and probably also in Alfred's Court and Back Pall Mall. Outside of that concentrated area, there were more in Parker Street and at the junction of Eaves Lane with Harpers Lane. There may have been smaller concentrations in other parts of the early town.

Of course, most of these old properties were overdue for demolition by the end of the 1950s and were cleared away. I was fortunate enough to see what they had been like before they disappeared. Fortunately, some examples remain in Parker Street.

Throughout the early 1950s, with World War Two not far behind us, reminders of that period remained abundant. Even the former air raid shelters could be seen in some places. Many of the deep ones, however, had had their entrances blocked, and in some cases had been covered altogether.

The residents of the Queens Road, Crown Street and Woodville Road had a common deep shelter, which was still in situ, with its entrance blocked. This was the place where I suppose, along with my parents, I had first been introduced to Mr Williams, whose house was quite close to the shelter. Stemming from that meeting, we visited sites of shelters in the early 1950s.

We even visited the former shelter which had been used by staff and pupils of the primary school at Hollinshead Street. The shelter, was built at the end of Stanley Street, which was then a cul-de-sac. The land is now used for parking by Borough Council employees working at the Civic Offices in Union Street.

Access to the shelter from the schoolyard was through a gateway, now bricked up but still visible. I recall that we used to have lessons in there at times. I suppose it was the same with other schools in Chorley. I often think it would be interesting to learn more about this time, when, as children, we understand so little of what was happening in the war.

But those lessons that we had in the shelter differed greatly from the normal lessons, because we had to wear our gas masks. It was a great excuse, in the poor lighting of the shelter, to make 'rude' noises by blowing into the gas mask while blocking the normal filter outlet with your hand. This produced a series of noises which caused us much amusement, but not , I'm afraid, to our teachers. Later visits to these sites were always reminders of those fun-filled lessons.

One of the deepest shelters was on the Coronation Recreation Ground in Devonshire Road, where a long, sloping ramp was often used by children for sliding down. That shelter still remains today, the entrance blocked, and the ramp filled in.

As well as former air-raid shelters, we visited places that the local Home Guard group used and those 1950s forays into what remained of the wartime buildings were rather poignant, in that it was recent history – still relatively fresh in the mind, yet little about the period in Chorley had been recorded. It was an important time in the social history of Chorley.

The whole of that period – the late 1940s and early 1950s – was particularly special for me. I even played a part in Chorley getting a mention on BBC radio's *Children's Hour*. At the Parish Church a team of young bell-ringers were learning the art, under Mr Gartside and Mr Rigby. It was discovered that the team were the youngest in Lancashire at the time. I happened to be the youngest of that team. We achieved some publicity via the local press, for a recording of us ringing was played on the radio.

It was in the early 1950s that I started my apprenticeship at Horwich Locomotive Works. Here I met with another like-minded person, who was interested in local history and archaeology, and brought my new friend

To show my early involvement as a Parish Church bell ringer, I include the above photograph dating from the late 1940s. It was taken as we were, at the time, the youngest team in Lancashire, and had rung for BBC Radio's *Children's Hour*. (Yours truly was the youngest of that team!). Pictured, back row, left to right; Keith Morris, Geoff Astin, Bill Burkey: front row, left to right; Gene Wareing, Joyce Williams, Jack Smith, Margaret Entwistle and Eric Greenhalgh.

Mr John Winstanley and Mr Williams together. From that beginning, we set up the first Chorley and District Archaeological Society in 1953. Our first public meeting was held in the former Reform Club in St George's Street. That infant society was soon making news, as we discovered many remains of prehistoric man's occupation of the local moors.

As boys we had a great scrapyard in Chorley at the bottom of Harpers Lane. This could be accessed easily from the back of the pub that used to be there, the Spinner's Arms. In this yard we found all types of machines, vehicles, and even aircraft parts which had been bought for scrap. Of course we often got chased out, but it was always worth going back again to obtain certain items to make 'canoes'. These were the long pod-shaped aircraft fuel tanks, which we cut in half to make our canoes. The canoes were always capsizing or sinking so deep water had to be avoided, but that yard remained a 'mecca' for many boys of the time.

I have referred, in previous books, to our early entrepreneurial dealings with the mill pond goldfish , whereby we would obtain the fish by netting, so as not to injure them, and sell them to local 'outlets'. Of course we always took a risk when this operation was under way, for we never had permission to net the fish ,or even to be on that land. One of the ironies about this money-raising enterprise, was that the best mill lodges to get the fish from were the hardest to approach.

Some of the cotton mill lodges where fish were caught were at Primrose Mill, Friday Street, and Fletchers Mill, off Lyons Lane. We often tried for goldfish at Brown's Mill off Brown Street, and at Smethursts North Street Mill, but without success, although other types of fish were found in these two lodges.

Money was always in short supply to lads of the time. After all, we would be hoping to go to the pictures at least twice a week, sometimes even three or four times. The problem could often be countered seasonally, with jobs like potato picking – a job which has probably gone by now – or helping out at hay time on local farms or even mowing lawns, but that was very hard work. There were no 'Flymos' or other electric mowers and few could afford a petrol-powered one in those days.

The detailed notes I made during the 1950s have been a great source of information for my previous books on that decade and, I am told, that details of some events and activities have stimulated much controversy and argument. My historian colleague Mr Williams also showed me how interesting some of the commonplace children's games and rhymes were, in that they were often historical in context. This was often something of a revelation, for some of them were a little bit 'risqué'. Many of the local girls seem to have made up their own words to many of them, and local people were often the subject of the skipping rhyme.

The street games played in the 1950s were somewhat dependent on the lighting we had, which, at that time was gas-powered and gave only poor illumination. Thus games such as 'Kick the Can', 'Tig in the Den' and 'Hide-and-Seek' were favourites. The lamp posts themselves could be easily converted into a swing, with a length of rope hung from the ladder arm of the lamp. Other games usually entailed the use of a ball and someone's house gable end, until we were told to go away by the householder, who had got fed up with the 'bump, bump' of the ball on the wall of their house. There was, of course, the ever-popular hopscotch. The chalked outline of the game's layout was a familiar sight on pavements everywhere. This is, of course, one game which remains popular, though little did we imagine that future generations would enjoy the game at school, the course permanently painted on the playground floor, as if to give it an 'official' mandate. Sadly, nowadays, it is rarely seen chalked on the flags outside of school.

I wonder how many generations of readers remember the game we played across the width of the street, called 'Statues'? One person turned to the wall at one side and those playing crept across the street? The person facing the wall would turn, and if he/she saw anyone moving they would have to go back to the other side of the street. You had to become a 'statue'. Usually this ended up with arguments about who was moving and who wasn't. This was one of the mixed games we played. The boys would even have a go at some of the girls' skipping games more out of bravado than anything else – but could never match the skills the girls had.

One of the most popular boys' games was called 'Trust'. It was a team game, where one team crouched down in line, and the other team vaulted over their backs to get up to the front of the crouching team. If the crouchers held the team up on their backs for long enough they won, and they took their turn to jump. If they collapsed, they had to be the crouching team again. This was a dangerous game where the crouching team usually suffered injuries to legs or heads from "flying boys" clogs or boots.

I think that apart from the seasonal games like football, cricket and sledging, and the things like tree-climbing, jumping rivers, damming rivers, making camp fires and so on, the favourite game was that of 'Knock the Door', where you knocked on someone's door and ran away. But we took it to a finer art than its basic form. The door selected had to have an entry opposite to it, and we would tie a fine thread to the knocker, move into concealment across the street, and pull the thread to lift the knocker.

This was repeatable, until discovery, when running was the only means of escape. You were always 'on the edge' in this game.

Even this became jaded, so we selected adjoining houses, perhaps in a terraced row, and tied the knockers together, allowing a little bit of slack. Then we knocked on both doors. Here too it was a laugh a minute until the householder came from the back of the house, when it was time for urgent evacuation.

As we have just talked about games for boys, I am reminded about how boys in the 1950s did bravado tasks, which were a little more than games. To prove the tasks had been completed it was necessary to have a witness or to leave some proof behind. Most of these bravado tasks involved climbing. Buildings (especially those cloaked in scaffold), filled gas holders, like the ones at the Bengal Street Depot, and factory chimneys, if a steeplejack was at work and had left his ladders in place were particularly popular. Often the bottom of these were covered by a plank and negotiating the planked lower section was considered part of the task.

Often these tasks were done under cover of darkness, which made them doubly dangerous, but added to the excitement. Also popular were the fire escapes, where you could sneak a look at what was going on in some top-floor rooms. The fire escape behind the Royal Oak was a favourite for this, because you could see into the function room. Of course, it was being seen which caused the real adrenalin rush, as you ran to evade capture.

There was one instance when there was scaffolding around the old police station. Climbing up that scaffold and leaving a marker was the sort of bravado test that earned just about the ultimate in points. I can, however, say that this challenge was carried out with great satisfaction, and no one got caught either.

For me the early to mid-1950s was a time of learning an apprenticeship and travelling back and forth to Horwich. Yet there was still time for escapism… for me this was the study of history and archaeology, with plenty of time spent on the local moorland looking for flint tools. But there were still a great many things to be noted about what was happening in and around the town.

The year 1955 seems to have been a particularly notable year. Take, for example, those heavy snowfalls in January and February 1955, when some of the local townships were cut off for a time. Great for sledging and fun, but not so good for getting about or to work, with buses being unable to get to many outlying places, especially in the Wheelton, Withnell, Heapey and Rivington areas.

At just about the time when the heavy snow was clearing, at the end of February 1955, one of the first television celebrities visited Chorley. This was a chap called Macdonald Hobley, who had been 'Announcer of the Year' on the television during 1953–4. He was in Chorley to chair a 'Brains Trust' parlour game in the Town Hall. This was based on a favourite television show at this time.

April 1955 was a time for concern for many cinemagoers in Chorley. The Royal in Market Street had been closed. This was a cinema which usually showed two main films per week, yet its internal comfort and decor was somewhat lacking in 'modernity', shall we say. It was certainly a place which had character. After all, it had been built as the Theatre Royal in 1911.

I suppose the most often-remembered feature of the

Royal was its second balcony, the one nicknamed 'the monkey rack'. It was so steeply tiered that you almost had to hang on like a monkey. I have written, in earlier books, in detail about how we used to dangle paper on a length of thread from this location, and into the projector beam, so that it showed on the screen as a black moth-like image. But another thing we did – as it's confession time – was to take a little water up there as well – bottled of course. This was gently sprinkled down to the auditorium seating, which caused some consternation, and was usually the prime mover in getting us thrown out yet again, which was a regular thing. Happy memories.

The Royal had allegedly been closed for refurbishment, and we were not unduly worried. After all, we still had four more cinemas . During the last week of April 1955, those four cinemas were showing the following films: at the Odeon, *So This is Paris* and *Destry*; at the Empire, *The Adventures of Robinson Crusoe*; at the Pavilion it was *Saracen Blade*, and the Plaza were showing *Woman's World*. A varied selection from which to choose.

Speaking of cinema, remember how as boys (for I'm sure the girls would never get up to the tricks we did as boys) we would buy a cheap seat ticket at, say, one and six, then visit the toilets and move back into the dearer seats, often to be caught by the usherette? Or how we would let our mates in via the back doors if we didn't have enough money for us all to go and see the film? What about how we were not able to get into those 'A' category films without an adult, and how we stood outside asking strangers 'Can you take us in please?' Could you imagine that ever happening today?

Of the four cinemas listed above, three of the buildings survive into 2002. With the move back to the cinema, who knows, we could even see a resurrection of the multiplex at the former Plaza, but it seems more likely that a purpose-built new cinema would be built. But that is irrespective – the return of cinema to Chorley is long overdue.

Before leaving this look at the cinemas, an interesting item of news cropped up, pertaining to late April 1955. The Odeon was showing *The Colditz Story*. One of the stars of that great war film was Lionel Jeffries, who played the part of an Irish Guards officer. One of the VIP guests at the Odeon was a Mr B.W. Jeffries, the actor's father. He was the Superintendent of the Highways Hostel in Balshaw Lane.

During this time, the showing of films on a Sunday was one of the subjects being discussed in the local press. In fact there had been much discussion and publicity in the national media about the religious aspects of whether or not films should be shown at all on a Sunday. In many other Lancashire towns this subject was also being raised. During August a series of well-attended public meetings were held in the Town Hall Assembly Room, when arguments for and against the showing of Sunday films were heard. As can be imagined, clergy from churches in the town were regular attendees at these meetings. By November 1955, the results of a poll were made public. The announcement took place in the Town Hall, where many of the meetings had been held. The result showed a majority of 2,602 votes in favour of holding Sunday cinemas in Chorley.

Another change to daily life was the completion of Southlands School in August. The first headmaster appointed was Mr Townsend. In June 1955 I had revisited my old school at Hollinshead Street, where the wall of the gable end had fallen through the roof of the main hall. Fortunately this incident had taken place at the weekend, and no one was in the school at the time.

In the final month of the year, a couple of items caught my eye from notes of the time. First was an event held in Coppull, at the Oak Tree pub, where the pit brow women from the Welch Whittle Colliery attended a social evening. This colliery was one of the last in Lancashire to employ women. Needless to say, the ladies turned up much more elegantly dressed than their normal working attire of protective clothing and 'brats'.

Another event in December was one for the boys really, yet it was something that Chorley television viewers were quite proud of, for a local girl singer appeared on the *Carole Levis Talent Show*. It was the first time she had appeared on television, and she took the stage name of Trixie Margo. From time to time she sang at the Tudor Ballroom in Chorley, where she was greatly appreciated by the local lads.

Funny how, in the mid-1950s, as children we had territorial areas. We referred to 'our end', where we lived, and conversed with terms like 'up your end'. The lads on Eaves Lane had all the Nab to play around, where one could explore or climb in the quarry, or splash around in the 'Bluewaters', a former quarry by then full of water. 'Our end' was Astley Park, for several of my mates lived in houses adjoining the park railings, so we could access the park at any time.

Within our own 'end', I suppose we were rather 'parochial' in wanting to keep our surroundings as personal a place as we possibly could, for it was simply 'our' territory. Boys would automatically join the local gang of lads, as a matter of course. In October, when these gangs foraged for materials to make as big a bonfire as possible, we stood guard over it to make sure some of the material wasn't stolen, or set alight before 5 November.

We were armed to protect our bonfires and our territory, usually with a catapult, which we made ourselves, becoming au fait with its capabilities. Catapult ammunition was usually a supply of suitably-sized stones, but there was one particular type of ammunition which not only was more accurate, but was good for distance as well. This was the steel ball bearing.

The only place we could get these from was a car scrapyard or garage, which were not that common in the early to mid-1950s. One favoured place used to adjoin my primary school at Hollinshead Street. It was a scrapyard belonging to the garage of Messrs Hughlock Hindle & Co of Union Street. Finding the ball-bearing cases was difficult enough, but getting the actual ball-bearings out of their cases was even more difficult. It was a sort of team effort to get this special ammunition. We even had at least one girl who helped us get the bearings.

As far as having one's own territory was concerned, we made forays into different areas not only more of an adventure, but one with an element of risk, in case we were faced with opposition from rival gangs. During the mid-1950s, several areas in Chorley had poor housing which had been earmarked for demolition. These areas were often visited to see what we could find, and were somewhat like a raid into enemy territory.

In 1956, demolition of the first of the pre-selected sites began at Botany. Houses and a couple of pubs adjoining the canal bridge were also demolished, plus the infamous Long Row, which ran parallel to the canal on the Knowley Brow side. This was an area where troubles occurred, and where health visitors or anyone else in authority were not very welcome. This was probably one of the reasons that these were the first selected houses to be demolished.

The clearance continued through 1957 into 1958, when many of the old weavers' cottages had been removed in the Bolton Street, King Street and Standish

In Bolton Street the clearance of old property was well under way in the late 1950s, and these old shops were due to go very soon. They were on what is now the Ford car showrooms forecourt at the end of Standish Street.

Street areas. This also meant that the old Lodging House in King Street had to be cleared as well.

In the late 1950s we saw the first television broadcast from Chorley, when a boxing tournament was held in the Town Hall. The need for better television reception saw the building of a television mast on Winter Hill. It was easy to see the growing popularity of television sets in the home, with an increasing number of aerials appearing on chimney stacks. This blossoming television culture came with the emergence of teenagers. For the first time young people had their own favourite brand of dress, of entertainment and of dancing. It was, after all, the era of Rock 'n' Roll.

In the introduction to this book I said that many Chorley people had suggested how certain toys, games, books, household products and other items, bought in the 1950s, reminded them of that decade. Many of the shops are gone now, or have been rebuilt. To evoke a few memories of that decade, I include a chapter of photographs later, showing some of the shops that will

bring back a few memories. But here I would like to remind you of some of the typical products of the 1950s, as well as mentioning a few films that you might have seen. Or, if you had a television set in your house in the 1950s, what you might have been watching. I have consulted many local contemporaries of mine and what follows is a selection of what could be called 'favourite items from the 1950s.

We seem to have had a great number of comics, magazines and books in the 1950s, many based on popular television and radio shows, as more paper had become available following the relaxation of wartime paper shortages. There were a lot of annuals for children and you may remember some of the following: *Wagon Train Album, Kit Carson Annual, Radio Fun Annual, Television Fair Album, Television Comic Annual, Mr Pastry Annual, Lion Annual* and others. We bought comics such as *Topper, Beezer, Television Fun, Film Fun, Tiger, Bunty, School Friend*, and not forgetting the famous *Eagle*, with Dan Dare and his nemesis the Mekon. A girls' version of

In 1959, Bulloughs of Chorley gave the price of electrical goods in guineas. One guinea was £1 1s (£1.05).

Eagle came out as well. Do you recall what its name was? It was simply called *Girl,* and was similar to the *Eagle.* A junior version was called *Robin.*Incidentally, did you know that the *Eagle* had its origins and production in Southport? Our parents might have read magazines such as *John Bull* and *Vanity Fair.*

As for toys of the period, the boys had Dinky toys and Meccano sets. There were Bayco Building Sets, Minibrix sets and Mobo toys, plus games like Cluedo, and Subbuteo for table football fans. We had jigsaw puzzles galore, television games, space games and space toys.

We bought Dansette record players to listen to those singers of the time, such as Johnny Ray, Guy Mitchell, Petula Clark and Frankie Vaughan. At the pictures we might have seen *Reach for the Sky, Gentlemen Prefer Blondes, The Lavender Hill Mob, 20,000 Leagues Under the Sea, Ben Hur, El Cid, The Ten Commandments* and *Around the World in Eighty Days.* And when we went to the pictures, we bought film magazines such as *Picture Goer* or *PhotoPlay.* We listened to radios which had a large number of valves in them, and portable radios were the size of a shoebox and made by Bush, K.B., Philips or Ferguson.

Our parents bought the weekly shopping at the grocers. There were no supermarkets. More packaged goods were introduced during the 1950s. such as Tetley Tea Bags (1952), Puffed Wheat and Frosted Flakes (1954), Ricicles and Fish Fingers (1955). With the coming of the washing machine, we saw soap powders like Persil, Daz, Omo, Fab and Dreft. Nor can we forget some of the new sweets of the time, such as Crunchie, Bounty, Picnic, Opal Fruits, Spangles and many more. There were certain shops our parents

took us into, especially when we needed new clothes or shoes. Do you recall having your feet X-rayed? No doubt, this small selection of items will have helped you remember Chorley in the 1950s.

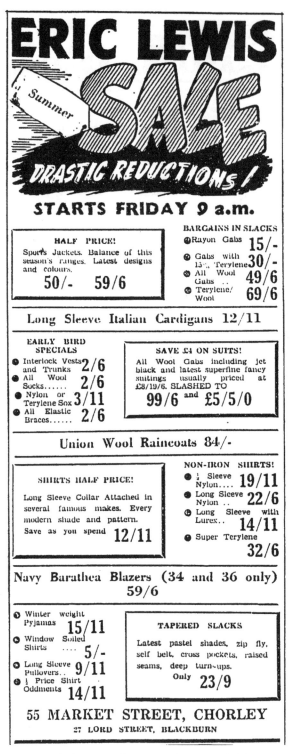

Eric Lewis's shop in Market Street, Chorley, was holding a sale of menswear in September 1958.

THE 1960S

DESPITE the opening of the Preston bypass in December 1958 – after a period of construction which had begun in June 1956 – the amount of traffic moving through Chorley along the A6 trunk road was still heavy. We had been told that when the new 'Birmingham-Preston Motor Road' was finished, Chorley would have a bypass road which would take all the through traffic away from the main streets'.

This proved to be totally incorrect. The new road did not take traffic away, especially between December 1958 and July 1963. In fact, since the Preston bypass had opened, more vehicles were coming through Market Street. It was the same in Euxton village, through which the A49 road runs. Traffic through the village had been as heavy as it was in Chorley.

What was happening, following the opening of the Preston bypass, was that to get on to that road, at Bamber Bridge, six miles to the north of Chorley, all traffic had to come through Chorley or Euxton. Thus the volume of traffic was increased. In addition to the normal traffic, as I mentioned in my introduction, many visitors were coming from the Midlands just to ride along the Preston bypass route. It was after all the first 'motor road'. For some five years or so it became a visitor attraction in itself.

The M6 motorway between Bamber Bridge and Cheshire, which included the huge viaduct over the Manchester Ship Canal at Thelwall, and, closer to Chorley, the Gathurst Viaduct, was opened on 29 July 1963. This was the section of 'motor road' which passed two miles to the west of Chorley, where we all expected the Chorley access slip roads to be built. But this did not happen. Instead a service station was built there, at Charnock Richard – one of Chorley's villages which is perhaps more widely known than Chorley itself because of those services.

To officially access or exit the M6 motorway, even today, almost 40 years since opening, one has to travel from Chorley, north to Leyland, or south to Standish. Although perhaps a minimal reduction of through traffic passing through Market Street was noted following

opening of the Preston to Cheshire section of the M6, it was not as great a reduction as was anticipated. It would be several years before the traffic could travel along the full length of the M6 motorway and actually reduce Chorley's traffic problem.

Apart from the concern regarding a motorway access link for Chorley in the town itself, the demolition of old property which had started towards the end of the 1950s continued throughout the 1960s. As I indicated in the introduction, imports of raw cotton and finished cotton goods were having an increasing effect on Lancashire mills in general, including those in the Chorley area. Some went on to short-time working, as orders were reduced or cancelled.

Since my previous notes about the 1960s in Chorley, several readers have reminded me of other events of the decade. It is, of course, impossible to discuss every event in detail. Nor will I assume that everything written previously has been read. So I shall touch upon some of those familiar events, as well as discussing at more length some of those which have been brought to my notice.

With the demolition of much of the older properties in Chorley, and the rehousing of residents, there were a number of pet cats who found their new accommodation less than 'acceptable'. They wandered away, to go in search of their old haunts. Some were never seen again. Happily, many of the cats were returned safely to their distressed owners, either by the local RSPCA or by former neighbours, who were still living in the area where demolition had taken place. I have been told how, after some weeks, one cat found its way from Tootell Street estate back to the Bolton Street area, across many busy streets, and was eventually reunited with its owner. Sadly some cats were unable to be rehoused in their owners' new homes and had to be 'put to sleep' at the Back Street depot, near the old Fire Station building.

Although, by the 1960s, the 'trial' lights had been made permanent, the Lyons Lane/Bolton Street crossroads was still an easy and popular place to watch the traffic, in the place referred to as 'up Duke'. Although there were no longer as many accidents and shunts to be seen there since the coming of the traffic lights, it remained a popular spot to watch, especially now that railings, great for leaning on, had been erected. Plus, of course, there were still several pubs close at hand.

I was told by one person, this past year, how a relative of theirs had been employed in a census of traffic moving out of Lyons Lane, before the lights were even erected temporarily. The census taker used one of those former watchman's huts to avoid the worst of the weather. Readers will probably remember those little huts – they looked a bit like a sentry box with a seat and were usually seen where roadworks were under way. They usually had a brazier fire in front of them, and were turned away from the wind to keep the watchmen warm. In those days, of course, the red warning lamps used paraffin.

As I mentioned in my introduction, June 1964 saw a proposal to build a multi-storey car park on the site of the Flat Iron market place. This was to be connected to a shopping precinct, which would have been built nearer to Clifford Street, along the length of the site, from the end of Hill Street almost to Union Street.

The shopping area would have been on two levels and completely covered. This was 30 years before the present-day shopping mall was built. In retrospect, the 1960s' scheme seems to have been a much better option, without the car park. At least we would have had a covered shopping mall instead of the 'long entry', uncovered precinct of Market Walk, that we have today.

I also mentioned in the introduction that, at the time of writing, the Flat Iron market site is again under threat. The proposed relocation of the bus station to a site near the railway station, latterly used for parking, will create a

During her tour of St Michael's School in 1965, Princess Margaret met many of the children as well as officials. She is seen here in one of the classrooms with two pupils.

shortage of parking spaces. The suggested new parking site is, once more, the Flat Iron market.

In 1965 Chorley entertained a special royal visitor. Princess Margaret came to officially open St Michael's School in Astley Road. Doubtless some readers will have been among those of us who waited for what seemed to be a very long time to see her. We were rewarded with the briefest of glances, as the great black cars swept past us and into the school driveway. Some of us did catch a glimpse of her as she got out of the car and went into the school. I was lucky enough to see the princess in London on two separate occasions, and at much closer quarters than I had in Chorley.

For teens and 20-something lads, growing up in Chorley during the 1960s, owning a motorbike meant greater freedom to travel. It was the time of 'Mods and Rockers' battles, which were so often shown in the newspapers and on the television news. As many readers will remember, the lads who owned scooters were the 'Mods' and those with motorbikes were 'Rockers'. Most of the fights seem to have been in the coastal towns of southern and eastern England, but I seem to recall that there were a few minor skirmishes in Blackpool, although nothing too serious.

The trouble with getting a motorbike was that you started with one with a small engine, say 125cc, but soon wanted one with a bigger engine. We would spend hours 'drooling' over used and new bikes at dealerships like Rogerson's in Chorley. A group of us gradually acquired bigger machines, and ran them quite fast in certain places. Those places were our 'test tracks', or perhaps they were our 'daredevil runs'. They were certainly our 'speed runs'.

The saying 'now it can be told' might be used at this point, I suppose for, 40 years ago, there were only three suitable places in the Chorley area to 'test' a bike to see what sort of speed it would reach. Before anyone comments that we were mad or reckless, let me say that we might have gone rather fast, but we did have a relatively safe system in operation when achieving those high speeds. There were not so many cars on the roads in those days, nor as many houses with associated road junctions and/or roundabouts leading to them. Also, the high speed runs were always done in 'no limit' areas.

We always used lookouts and a signal system and were considerate of other traffic on the two fastest routes. The third route was less fast than the other two, and you

would be lucky to get up to 80–90mph. On the faster routes you achieved speeds of up to 100mph and more, depending on the bike and traffic conditions. This was in the days before the motorways too.

Of the two fast runs, the fastest was along Blackrod bypass, where you had a long run with only one crossroads. The second fastest was along Euxton Lane. At the time there were no other main roads joining it, only a few lanes and the ROF main gate. The run extended from the railway bridge near the Bay Horse pub in Euxton to the top of Euxton Lane, at approximately what is now the entrance to the Chorley and Leyland District Hospital.

The slowest of the three ran from the end of Pepper Lane in Standish to Coppull Moor. Although this was only an 80mph route, it did pass the local café where the bikers met – at that time Lil's Café – so you usually did the run in front of an audience. It was certainly a morale booster and good for conversation later.

As I mentioned in the introduction, in 1966 work began on the new Preston-Manchester road, which was to become the M61. To accommodate the route of this new 'motor road' through Chorley, more houses had to be demolished in Botany, as well as the nine-arch railway viaduct carrying the Blackburn-Wigan line over the canal. The viaduct was demolished in 1969, when much of the work in the town itself took place. The people of Chorley were grateful that, at least, the road could be accessed from the town itself, though great changes to the Borough itself were more than apparent.

The new motorway passed through the Borough from the south through Anderton, then Heath Charnock, Chorley town, Whittle le Woods and Clayton le Woods to the north. The building of the road took away much of the local countryside, which can never be restored, but the Chorley section took travellers through some of the best countryside along the whole route of the M61.

I have devoted a photographic section showing aspects of building of the road, and in some cases, what certain areas were like before it was built. Most people will, perhaps, recall the demolition of the railway viaduct, but what of Bagganley Hall and 'Johnny's Brow'? I wonder how many readers took part in the sponsored walk along the M61, from Hartwood to Anderton and back, with the mayor, Adam Barnes, and Chorley Silver Band, to help raise funds for a day lounge at Chorley Hospital? That was

Pending demolition of the railway viaduct in Botany, this photograph was also taken from the top of it in November 1968. It looks towards Thornhill and also shows the temporary timber and rubble decking that covered the canal, to stop the viaduct masonry falling into it.

in late 1969, shortly before the northern section of the road was opened.

Interestingly, someone had quoted a local councillor from the 1950s who had said, somewhat sarcastically, following all the hype about the bypass routes for Chorley, that 'man would walk on the Moon before Chorley got a bypass'. However sarcastic that prediction, it proved accurate, for while July 1969 saw humanity's first steps on the Moon, it was 1970 before the new road opened.

But the road building didn't end there. In the 1990s a town centre bypass was constructed, and in 2001 and 2002 we have witnessed the destruction of Walletts Wood and River Yarrow water meadows, to create yet another bypass, this time to ease traffic problems of those living on a road (Collingwood Road) which itself had been built as a bypass. This constant road-building has lead many Chorley residents to wonder whether the town might be trying to break a record.

Wholesale redevelopment of Chorley town itself continued apace. In 1965 the police station made a temporary home at Woodlands Hostel, until a new station was completed by 1968. A photograph in the section 'People and Events' shows a line-up of new Ford Anglia Panda cars, with their drivers by them. This was taken at Woodlands Hostel site.

1966 saw the old gasworks in Water Street demolished – the site was later used as Chorley Teacher Training College, which was previously occupying the former grammar-school in Union Street along with large huts in Hollinshead Street. The former gasworks' offices were used by the college for lectures, etc.

As the college expanded, even these new premises became too small. The college had been using the huts in Hollinshead Street, plus the old gasworks' offices, some of the small houses adjoining the gasworks site, the former Parish Institute on Park Road, the Barracks in Devonshire Road and the former Hollinshead Street School. It was hardly surprising that they had to relocate. The new site was Woodlands Hostel.

The late 1960s saw the removal of Haydocks timber merchants in Clifford Street, and there was some controversy as to whether the works itself would be demolished, but the building was given a new lease of life being converted to for use as a supermarket. In later years this was taken over by Morrison's. Originally it was a

ground-level store only, and was somewhat claustrophobic. The new owners created an upper floor, which solved this problem.

Moving towards the 1970s, it was noticeable that the decline of the cotton manufacturing industry continued as it had all through the 1960s. Many local mills in and around Chorley went on short-time work or closed down altogether. Some mills saw small workshop units being set up in them which remain to this day, but not all the mills were suitable for this. Usually the former ground floor weaving shed was favoured over the multi-storey spinning mills. This was because ground floor mills were easier to access and maintain.

Some of the changes on the local industrial front in Chorley during the 1960s included Messrs Ashton Brothers' 1965 takeover of Talbot Mill and Gainsborough Cornard's takeover of Victoria Mill off Lyons Lane in 1965–6 where they installed modern machinery producing knitted goods.

In 1966, after several years of weaving towels, the company once referred to as Chortex, who occupied the multi-storey Brown Street Mill, merged with a Manchester company who ran Victoria Mill in Horwich. Production at Chorley was run down and eventually transferred to Horwich, where today, 35 years later, the name Chortex is still displayed at the Horwich mill.

Again in 1966, Chorley bleach works, at Common Bank, installed new machinery costing some £100,000 to improve the efficiency of their dyeing and bleaching methods. By this time, much of the yarn and cloth being processed at many bleach works was man-made. The popularity of man-made fibres had continued to increase since its introduction.

In 1969, the Gainsborough Cornard knitwear company of Victoria Mill needed to expand and modernise their processing departments. To the south side of the factory was a large open space, which, it was assumed, would be the site for the extension to the works. However, permission to build on this large site, which lay vacant, was refused by the local planning authority. An alternative site for the expanded works was offered to the company, outside of Chorley, but this proved unsuitable. It would have necessitated many changes in their production methods at the existing Victoria Mill, and additional costs in moving goods between the two sites.

It was hardly surprising, then, that the company

declined the offer and announced it was to close the Chorley works and relocate its entire business to Ireland. The mill was subsequently occupied by Pennine Cleaners. Today the site of Victoria Mill has become that of Morrison's supermarket – its tall chimney the single reminder of the past history of the mill. When the chimney was threatened by demolition, I joined others in ensuring its preservation.

The land beside the old mill, the site of the proposed extension to the Gainsborough Cornard works, is now the supermarket car park and one wonders why it was unsuitable all those years ago. Had the extension had been permitted, the company may still have been producing knitwear in Chorley.

The closures of the mills did not end with Victoria Mill. In 1969–70 Messrs Stuttards Mill also closed, and Carrington and Dewhurst in Eccleston went on short-time

due to lack of orders. Short-time work had become one of the precursors to closure of many mills in Lancashire. It was something we would see more of in the 1970s.

During the 1960s, many of the shops and, in particular, their frontages, in and around the town centre were given a facelift. Often these alterations resulted from much-needed repair work, which in turn led to modernisation. Most of this was typical of the transformations appearing up and down the country at that time and resulted, all too often, in a 'sameness' when many of our shops lost their individuality and character. Many shops were transformed when they passed into the hands of new owners after many years in the ownership of one family. The new proprietors often found the traditional premises a bit old-fashioned and so modernisation was in order.

In my later chapter 'Remember These Shops.', in the photographic section, you will see some of those old-style

St Thomas's Road looking to the end of Dole Lane, with the Rose and Crown pub to the left in the early 1960s. The shops were Regent sweet shop by Dole Lane, next was Strangward's electrical goods, then Sumner's milliners, with Thompson's tailors above.

shops. But for now I would like to remind you of some of the familiar items we bought there.

Where did we get our toys from in the 1960s? There were not very many toy shops in Chorley then, were there? What were we getting as presents? Some of the most popular toys of the decade were 'spacehoppers', which you sat on and bounced around holding on to two ear-like handles. Not forgetting British-born Sindy and her American rival Barbie who had little sister Skipper and boyfriend Ken, and Tressie with hair that grew at the touch of a button.

How about the improved Scalextric sets? How much better were they in the 1960s than they had been in the late 1950s? Wasn't it amazing just how many 'space' things there were, from full spacesuits, to ray guns and robots of all shapes and sizes? We saw a return of more metal toys, but a huge number of them were made from plastic.

Television had become more popular in the early 1960s, especially for children. More and more television time was devoted to programmes especially aimed at children, and all ages were catered for. Many of the shows had been airing since the 1950s, and some were repeats from that decade. Do you remember shows like *Pinky and Perky* and *The Singing Ringing Tree*, or *The Adventures of Tin Tin*? What about *Captain Pugwash*?

Television continued to influence much of our reading – we read less, went out less and watched television more. For children of the 1960s, the spin-off in annuals based on television shows was very dominant. *Danger Man*, *The Man from Uncle*, and *Softly Softly* – all police or spy programmes on television each produced popular annuals. There were a great many more for all ages, such as the *Coronation Street* annual *Daktari* and *Dr Kildare*, plus the *Rupert* annual, which remains as popular today as it was then. For the boys there was *Joe 90*, *Stingray*, *Fireball XL5*, *Thunderbirds* and *Dr Who*. The girls might have opened *June*, *Pippin*, *Twinkle*, *Mandy* and *Sparkle*. There was also the Tufty Club annual. The Tufty Club, of course, was an early attempt to instill road safety rules in the minds of the under-fives. Our parents read *Annabel*, *Petticoat*, *Penthouse*, *Private Eye*, *Which* and *Punch*, some of which continue to this day. Late teens and 20-somethings might have been reading *19*, *Honey* and *Twiggy*.

The music played on our transistor radios was now

Moores of Market Street had a big sale of boys' and menswear in June 1962.

less for adults, and had started to cater for teenagers, and there was one special import from the USA – the jukebox – which will always be associated with 1960s music, especially Rock 'n' Roll. Jukeboxes were appearing in

In September 1962, Leslies furniture shop advertised a three-piece suite for £38 – and you could buy it 'on tick' if you wished.

The local Co-op offered an interesting range of goods in this August 1962 advertisement – everything from soup and jam to toilet soap and wax polish.

coffee bars, clubs and pubs all over Chorley.

It was not just the American artists who were favourites then. There were our home-grown stars, such as Cliff Richard, Billy Fury and Adam Faith, and groups like The Beatles, Gerry and the Pacemakers, The Shadows, Johnny Kid and the Pirates and The Rolling Stones. Among the most popular girl singers were Helen Shapiro, Cilla Black and Petula Clark. There is so much more I could write on this subject, so many memories to recall.

In just discussing the 1960s generally, remember how the Chorley newsagents gave such great coverage of important news items on their billboards? How about the football World Cup win by England in 1966? That was something to remember. Also making news, as a huge scandal, was the case of the minister John Profumo and a lady called Christine Keeler. That was in 1963. That year there was also the Great Train Robbery. But for me, it was the memorable late-night television, with the live broadcast of men walking on the Moon in July 1969. That must be a memory that cannot be bettered.

To end our discussion about Chorley during the 1960s

– of which I can only write in general terms, as space does not permit much more nostalgic memories – let us end this section with more shopping memories. What we were buying, for instance, at the grocers, supermarket? Slimming aids were commonplace, such as Limmits, Bisks, and Slimbread, and the decade saw the rise in the popularity of yoghurts with fruit.

'Ready-meals' became more available, and more foreign foods could be found on supermarket shelves. Then there were the ice creams and ice lollies. Remember Zooms and Splits? There were more drinks available in cans and plastic bottles, which saw the start of a litter problem, but also led to calls for recycling.

But, to end on a personal note, I still recall those special shops of the early to mid-1960s in Chorley, where our parents had been shopping for years, and, as a child, you were usually given a treat on each visit. Perhaps a sweet, a piece of cheese or malt bread, as you soaked up the sights and smells of those many shops. Shops such as the Maypole, and Dunderdale's, where they still patted the butter and ground coffee beans, and Booth's, where coffee smells dominated the air as it was freshly ground. How about the many bakeries, with the smells of freshly-baked bread? There are many memories recalled by discussing Chorley shops. I hope that writing about them here has recalled a few of them.

As we entered the 1970s, we were told that we were becoming a more 'global society'. We were thinking of what changes in our lifestyle might be ahead of us within such a society, where we would see foods common worldwide being available at our corner shops, and where world news would be reported 'live' with the launching of more satellites. Television was changing our lives, and we became more aware of events, in a world that got much smaller, as more of us flew off to distant holiday locations.

THE 1970S

AT the end of each decade, there are always a number of proposals, events and other activities or concerns which are ongoing, and overlap into the next decade. This was just the case with the passage of the 1960s into the 70s. I will not prioritise all the concerns that were felt in and around Chorley at this time. That would not be feasible in so small a volume, but some of those concerns and worries, which were based on newspaper reports published during the late 1960s decade, were as follows.

During this time we were made more aware of what damage was being done to our environment, and of basic moves to decrease pollution. We became more concerned with our planet's environmental issues generally. In addition to the reduction of open coal fires and mill chimneys, the introduction of smokeless fuels and smoke-free zones was a move towards more control over pollution. Throughout Lancashire, many rivers, especially those flowing through industrial towns, were badly polluted, including many in the Chorley area. During 1969, a comprehensive survey of rivers in the Chorley and district area was started, along with surveys of all the rivers around the county. It was anticipated that the results of this survey would only be completed in late 1970.

For some years a new town had been proposed in Central Lancashire. According to the media, this was to accommodate Manchester's overspill population. This new town, we heard, was to be based in and around the Chorley and Eccleston area and, although this idea was abandoned, its spectre was resurrected in the late 1960s, when another new town proposal became public. This proposal was to be based around Preston, Leyland and Chorley and, unlike its predecessor, it was not abandoned. Instead, offices for those who would be involved with this work were established in Leyland, and gradually, via the media, the proposals for this new development of our local countryside emerged.

In Chorley, the coming of the M61 motorway, had disturbed some of the water table levels of the River Chor in Cabbage Hall Fields, and compensation work was done, to ensure that the river still had a reasonable flow along its length. Additional drainage was run from the M61 to the river risings area, and changes were made to field drainage and ditches to ensure an adequate supply to the river. But when the river suddenly stopped flowing into Astley Park in 1969, and only a trickle was emerging, it was time for the borough engineer to answer many questions concerning the River Chor, and its flow, especially as many alterations had already been made to prevent such difficulties. The borough engineer's investigations revealed that the River Chor's reduced flow, as noticeable in Astley Park, was the result of some of the water having been diverted via a large-diameter pipe to supply water to a works lodge.

Our thoughts during early 1970s were quite jumbled, when it came to deciding how much land would be needed for the building of the new town, and where precisely this building was to be done. We were concerned with the closing of many local footpaths, not only within the new town designated area, but on Chorley Nab, where quarrying had left a huge scar, with many footpaths diverted 'temporarily'.

But what of the everyday events of the time? Just what do you recall that was topical or making news during the 1970s as a whole? In 1970 the former Gillibrand Hall Farm had been demolished and the site levelled. But the fate of the stone barn at the farm hung in the balance. It was dated 1669, was of historical and architectural interest and was a listed building, but it was in poor condition.

After it had been empty for some time, a group was formed, mostly of businessmen and arts-orientated people, with a view to creating an arts centre for Chorley at Gillibrand Farm Barn, which was only a short way from the hall itself. The local Historical and Archaeological Society contacted many potential supporters in an effort to safeguard the old barn, in case the 'Arts' proposal came to nothing. In July 1970, an Arts Trust was formed, which drew up proposals for the conversion of the stone barn, to become an exhibition centre.

The old mill above the canal bridge on Cowling Road had recently been vacated by Preston Farmers, and soon fell prey to local vandals, as did Crosse Hall Mill house and farm itself, as soon as it was vacated. Local Chorley vandals really are the best, I'm sure. (Even today, look at how Talbot Mill has been reduced to a shell in just one year).

Does anyone recall seeing the Wheelton Boat Club clearing weeds from the canal during September 1970? There were some sights to see on these events, when life jackets were the order of the day in case anyone fell into the canal. Talk about don't rock the boat. I think a few of those spartan weed removers might have had one for the road at times.

By October 1970, there was another complaint about the River Chor. This time, it was not the flow of water along it, but the smell coming from it. This was only noticeable when it emerged in the park, where it was seen to be discoloured also. The River Chor goes underground at Harpers Lane. It was thought that some underground contamination was the problem, which led to a large excavation taking place in Water Street, near its junction with Bengal Street, where subsidence problems had occurred in the past.

That same October saw a far more pleasing side to life in Chorley. Employees at the Friday Street Slipper Factory were the only people in Chorley to see a rather special visitor who came to the factory – Miss Great Britain, Kathleen Winstanley.

November 1970 saw the death of Mr George Marsden of Scawfell Road. Mr Marsden was a keen amateur astronomer. He was a member of many astronomical associations, and was always very patient with people who were also interested in astronomy – including myself – who spent much time learning about the subject from him.

From Harpers Lane you turn into Water Street, and here, viewed from the end of Commercial Road, we look back to the former main offices of T. Witter and Co. To the right, the Commercial pub. The works and pub are now demolished. Photograph dates from the late 1970s.

Also in November, an application by Messrs Tesco supermarkets caused an upset to many Chorley people. This was to convert the old Odeon cinema into a supermarket. There followed many articles in the local press about this proposal, with many other counter-proposals. A lot of the alternative proposals came from local people interviewed by the local press. Some of the most interesting counter-proposals included creating a dance centre catering for the young and old, making the building into a dance hall and cinema, creating a sports centre, or a shopping complex with a cinema. At the beginning of December, the Odeon saga still rumbled on, with much continued publicity in the media. Around this time, though, it was suggested that to build yet another supermarket, especially across from the town's principal building, the Town Hall, would be totally unsuitable.

Despite the controversy, the first week in February was one which local cinemagoers will always remember. The Odeon was to show its last film before closing as a cinema. as a cinema. That last film was the James Bond movie, *On Her Majesty's Secret Service.* The cinema has served the local community for 33 years, having been opened in February 1938. VIP guests had attended the opening, and a lavish brochure was prepared for the event. A page boy of that time was Mr J.G. Green, who went on to become manager there. He was still at the Odeon in 1959, when the cinema celebrated its 21st birthday.

Most of January 1971 seemed to have been taken up with proposals in the pipeline for the development of land in and around the district. There was great speculation about just how much land would be needed by the developers. Many farmers in Chorley townships were becoming apprehensive as to whether or not their land would be needed. This uncertainty caused a great deal of concern.

During March and April, we saw the new town officers move from their scattered locations to Cuerden Hall, although an office was retained in Leyland. The officials were now being called the Central Lancashire Development Corporation (CLDC), a name of which we would hear a great deal in the years to come. By June, reports in the press told of meetings with CLDC management, of visits to places in the area and of surveyors, and the first sketch plans also started to emerge in the press.

At the 1971 Chorley Carnival we saw a well-known band leader. Remember who this was? It was, of course, Joe Loss, who toured the town in the procession – something which doesn't seem to be done nowadays. The VIP guest now just appears on the carnival field. The Carnival Queen that year was Carole Warburton.

This was also a time when an awareness arose of the potential dangers of former mill lodges, many of which now had little or no water in them or were part-filled with rubbish. Not only were they becoming an eyesore, but they were also thought to be a hazard. They had also, of course, become redundant, and the area taken up by them could by now be put to better use.

A great many boys in Chorley spent many happy hours close by those mill lodges. I know I have spoken about the goldfish scam we were involved with, but some of them were also places where we built rafts to sail on, or made 'canoes' from those aircraft fuel tanks that we would 'obtain' from Messrs Hitchen's scrapyard. There was one old lodge that had been filled with rubble for many years, even in the 1960s, but still retained water and pondweed, and was full of newts. This was the mill lodge in Duke Street, which was used by the former cotton spinning mill of Nixon & Killick, who ran Moor Mill.

Birkacre lodge was one of the favourite spots to learn to swim, as the water here was not too deep. Another attraction were the car inner tubes we could get from a nearby scrapyard, and which we used as lifebelts. Another favourite lodge was that of Lower Healey. This is still the same in 2002. Most of the other mill lodges – at North Street, Friday Street, Yarrow, Progress, Standish Street and Brown Street – were all much smaller, and were not quite as easily accessed as the previous two mentioned. But they were all right for fishing, you know, especially right next to the 'NO FISHING' signs that were usually placed on their banks.

Of course, the reason for the lodges having become derelict and overgrown was that they were a relic of the steam age, needed when the mills were driven by steam engines, which required a supply of steam provided by the boilers, which in turn needed the water in the lodges. Sometimes, in the case of Birkacre and Lower Healey, more water was needed as part of the bleaching and dyeing work that was done by those works.

Many of the Chorley mills saw their driving steam engines superseded by direct drive from electric motors in the 1950s, although some continued in use into the 1960s, when the last of them was used. Up to their retirement, many of these steam engines were in perfect working order, and tears were shed when demolition men moved into those engine rooms, for they were so clean – a credit to the 'tenters' who looked after them.

Although we didn't realise it in October 1971, a saga was about to unfold which certainly made the headlines, and even television. It happened in Clayton. At first, it was thought that the proposal to create a sort of amusement complex, with swimming pool, children's play areas, boating, a dance hall, shops, gardens and even hovercraft racing was a good idea, but there were many people who were against the proposal. On top of which, many local societies, including Leyland Historical Society and the Chorley Historical and Archaeological Society, were very much against the proposal because the location for this proposed complex was at the 17th-century moated site of Clayton Hall Farm.

At this time, I was active with the recording of Chorley's old buildings, many of them being, supposedly, protected due to their being listed. I was finding that many of these buildings were in a very poor state of repair. Because of this, I was getting quite a lot of publicity in the media anyway, but when the Clayton Hall proposals came out, I was being interviewed and quoted extensively. We were not to know at that time that what was to happen to the hall farm, in the not too distant future, this was something that could not have been envisaged by any of us, but we'll return to that later on.

Perhaps some readers, like me, were at the official opening of the M61 services centre at Anderton, which also took place in October 1971. It was, after all, rather a special day. Her Majesty the Queen, was met by the Lord Lieutenant of Lancashire and I was fortunate to be only a short distance from her as she walked past in a red coat wearing a red and white hat to match. After opening the service station, she left by car to Leyland, where the royal train was waiting. I'm not too sure precisely which way the royal car travelled to Leyland, for the M61 was open of course – unless the cars were allowed to turn from M61 to M6, then to Leyland. Or, perhaps the royal car and escorts came off the M61 at Hartwood? Perhaps someone reading this will know. In either case, the Queen must have actually gone through Chorley itself.

Proposals for the future development of Withnell Fold were in the press during mid-December, when plans were announced to demolish the old paper mill – which had been the reason for the building of Withnell Fold village – and to develop the site. The outline proposals led to many meetings of the Urban District Council of the time, as well as residents' groups, who were concerned about exactly what would be happening to their village.

Towards the end of the year – again in the larger Borough – Withnell Silk Mill closed with the loss of many jobs. Also, at the end of December, the spinning and weaving mill in Abbey Village closed. Called Abbey Mill, its closure made a total of 240 people redundant.

In early January 1972, after two years of study, a report on the poor state of rivers in the North West was finally published by the Department of the Environment. This highlighted the level of pollution in our rivers according to a colour code, and it made surprising reading, for many of those rivers affected were local ones.

Perhaps you may recall the earth tremor that we felt in Chorley on 9 March, along with many other towns in north-west England. It happened at about 7am. I remember it felt a bit like a heavy vehicle was passing by, with a slight sideways movement as well.

None of us realised what it actually was. We just didn't associate it with being an earth tremor – not until it was reported as such on the radio and television. Like many other people, I had felt tremors in Italy and such places, but it was simply something that didn't happen in Chorley, was it? At least that's what we always thought. But it was not the first one that had been felt in the town.

In March and April 1972, members of the local Historical and Archaeological Society were liaising with the CLDC at Cuerden Hall, to carry out certain survey works on sites of potential historical interest in the area, as well as requesting that blue plaques be affixed to some of the buildings in Chorley, to commemorate their historical associations. One of the buildings to which the society intended to affix a plaque was the Trustee Savings Bank on Park Road, which had associations with Henry Tate. Although the CLDC was sympathetic to the proposals, and said that they applauded our concern, they were not forthcoming in handing out money for plaques. At least the society tried to get some recognition for the town's historical buildings. As you will read later, many of the Historical Society members joined the newly-formed Chorley Civic Trust which, it was hoped, would lead to better support for improving concern for the town's

In June of 1972, another royal visitor quite literally 'dropped in', by helicopter! The royal visitor was Prince Philip, who had come to open Norweb's Daniel Training Centre in Little Carr Lane. He is seen here chatting with local people.

historical buildings and civic amenities. There will be more on this later.

Having perhaps reminded a few people of when the Queen came to Anderton, a few paragraphs ago, what about the time when Prince Philip came to Chorley by helicopter? Do you remember what that visit was for? It was June 1972 and the helicopter landed on the lawned area surrounding a new college that had been built by Norweb. Quite a crowd had gathered to see him, expecting just a distant glimpse. It was a bit of a surprise when, after landing, he came over to the crowd and did a walkabout, chatting to many Chorley people .

The college was to be a training centre for electrical apprentices, and would instruct students on the maintenance of high voltage pylons. A row of short pylons, having full-sized tops, but not as high as the real ones, stretched across part of the grounds. This of course, as you all remembered I'm sure, was at the Daniel Training Centre, located off Little Carr Lane.

But it was the opening of the newest town centre pub which caused, perhaps, the greatest stir at the time. In 1972, many people still remembered the old pub demolished in the early 1960s, at the end of Mealhouse Lane. A new pub being built on the site neared completion by June that year, and the proposed name for it came as a surprise to many. The reason for the surprise was that everyone assumed the new pub would be called the Red Lion after its predecessor, but instead it was named the White Hart. One of the reasons that some people thought it might be renamed the Red Lion, was that that pub had associations with the days of the stage coach, which also stopped at two further town centre pubs – the Royal Oak and the Gillibrand Arms, which was on the site of the present Town Hall. The pub has become the White Hart again in 2002.

By 1972 the many years of smoke pollution had become very obvious on some of the main buildings in Chorley. Their stone or brickwork was blackened with this pollution, and, as I have mentioned environmental issues were now coming more to the fore. There was an awareness that a clean environment was the only way forward. With this in mind, a cost estimate was carried out on the principal buildings in the town which needed to be cleaned. These were the Town Hall, the Parish Church, St George's Church, St Mary's Church, Park Street Chapel, Park Road Chapel, Hollinshead Street Chapel, St Peter's Church and Astley Hall, as well as the front entrance gates to Astley Park. The cost to clean these buildings came to £50,000.

Remember how the area between Crosse Hall Fold and Froom Street used to be a special area for those of us who were children in the 1950s? You could walk on a path alongside Crosse Hall Farm and look inside the shippon at milking time. Then walk by (or perhaps paddle in) the rushpit before we arriving at Crosse Hall Mill Farm.

On the Froom Street side of the farm was a big detached house which used to be referred to as 'Mill House'. Whether that was its real name I'm not sure, but, when the farm and the house were vacated, it was ruined by vandals in double-quick time. Then the M61 came in the 1960s, to cut through the rushpit site, and the water supply to the pit was altered from its original route. The rushpit was filled with overflow water from Chorley Water Works, higher up the Nab. The 1970s certainly saw a change to this former pleasant area, one which has an interesting history and a water mill that dated back to the 17th century, as established by the Crosse family of Crosse Hall.

The area, by 2002, has gone from bad to worse, and house building seems to have priority, destroying more of the amenities that we used to have in Chorley. Most missed is the simple joy of being able to walk in pleasant countryside, like that between Crosse Hall Fold, Bagganley Hall, Temple Fields and White Coppice.

During September, the troubles that were going on in Northern Ireland were brought home to us in Chorley, when we saw the burial of a Chorley man who had been injured in the province and had subsequently died. He was Kingsman Roy Christopher. Before joining the army he had worked in my department at Cowling Mill, in the employ of Messrs T. Witter and Co.

Towards the end of the year we saw a lot of media coverage about the Odeon building once again, almost a year after its closure. Still nothing was happening there. The rumours were rife, as was the speculation about its future. Again a rather contentious point was raised concerning any redevelopment plans for the building. Consideration would have to be given to the Odeon's location, directly across from the Town Hall. This saga was to continue into the new year.

During the first week of January 1973, the Chorley RUFC played its first game at Limbrick Sports Field. This was something new to go and watch. The Chorley side played against Orrell, and won 19–9, which was a great introduction for the new team. The same week, Chorley FC won their game 5–0. It was a good week for local supporters.

1973, if you recall, was pronounced European Tree Planting Year. I knew you would all remember that. This may have been why the Central Lancashire Development Corporation or CLDC, based now at Cuerden Hall, decided to establish a tree nursery for the new town area in Charnock Richard.

The trouble with this proposal was that the location for this new nursery was to be on a site of great historical importance. It was one which the local Historical and Archaeological Society, were in the process of surveying and photographing, as well as raising awareness in the importance of the site from both a historical and archaeological point of view. The site was at Commissary Farm, off Back Lane. Not only was the farmhouse circa the 17th century or earlier, it was also a complete timber-framed building. The adjoining barn was of Cruck construction (like Rivington Barns), and probably of an earlier date. The building was surveyed by myself, and some of the farmhouse timbers were removed for future display by Stanley Street Museum at Preston. The buildings were demolished, but, as was revealed later, they need not have been, for the site was not levelled. 'Portakabins' were placed at the site, which used adjoining fields for the tree nursery. Those cabins were placed on or near the site of the old farmhouse, but the adjoining

Besides May Day events like maypole dancing on a green off Parker Street and Garden Street in 1978, a tree planting also took place during February 1979, when two rowan trees were planted by Mayor Albert Lowe. Here, we see Ross Hubbold steadying the tree, as the mayor plants it.

orchards to the back and front were not touched. They were still there in mid-2002.

In the 1970s, there was a follow-on to the removal of old property in the Bolton Street area, which had begun in the late 1950s and early 1960s, when more buildings were declared unfit, particularly around Critchley Street. Reminders of a proposal to create a leisure complex at Clayton Hall were paralleled in early 1973, when the media released details about how Park Hall was to get a makeover, to create an entertainment centre. On top of which, Park Hall itself was to be extended and developed as a hotel. Some of the proposals were to build a swimming pool (which could be covered for alternative use) and to build squash and tennis courts. One of the more intriguing proposals was to create a showjumping arena. There was even a possibility of boating on the lake.

The company who were proposing to do all this work were the same people who wanted to develop the Clayton Hall site. Park Hall had, for many years prior to the new owners, been a sort of Country Club owned by a Mr Few.

The Easter visits we all made to Rivington (as we still do today), which often meant a walk to the top of Rivington Pike itself, saw a change to our routine in 1973. This summit of the Pike, with its tower, was in such bad condition due to erosion and excess vandalism, that there was even a possibility that it might have to be demolished. It was estimated that to repair the tower and carry out remedial works to its foundations, would cost around £2,000. It was at this time that Rivington Pike Tower came under the control of Chorley Borough, who put out tenders for repair work to be carried out. During the Easter period, and for a time after Easter, the summit of the Pike was fenced off. Incidentally, Rivington Pike was known as 'Riven Pike' in the 16th century. It was one of the countrywide hilltops where warning beacons were lit during the coming of the Spanish Armada in 1588. The tower which is at the top of this high viewpoint today was built in the 18th century by the local squire.

On the point of tenders, I noted at the time that, as well as those for repairs to Rivington Pike Tower, the Rural District Council had also put out a notice for tenders to carry out modernisation to their older council houses in some of the local villages, such as Coppull, Clayton, Euxton and Whittle le Woods.

1973 was the year that the County Council took over the responsibility for local roads. This meant that the Borough Council, with its detailed knowledge of local problems, were no longer involved.

Another town bypass had been discussed many times by the local council, but in 1973 a bypass designed specifically for the town centre was under discussion. This was not the pre-war scheme which was to leave the A6 Bolton Road at Hoggs Lane, at Yarrow Bridge, then under the railway viaduct, passing to the east of Cowling Mill, Crosse Hall, Botany, to re-emerge at the Sea View on the A6 again. This time, the bypass was from Bolton Street, via Lyons Lane, re-emerging on to the A6 at the top of Preston Street at the Parkers Arms. However, much demolition of property was necessary for this scheme, which, it was envisaged, would be created within the next 15 years. Although we were unaware of the fine details of the town centre bypass proposal, the first phase of this may well have been the closure of Messrs Haydock's in Clifford Street, and the demolition of the long rows of old cottages on each side of Bengal Street. In late April 1973, we heard that a new prison was to be built in Ulnes Walton, on part of the former Ordnance Depot.

At Park Hall, alteration work to the complex was pressing ahead, and the showjumping arena would, it was hoped, be open by June, so that the first large equestrian event could be held there. This would be the Dunhill Northern Horse Jumping Championships. In fact, we were able to go and watch the horse jumping at the new Arena North at the Park Hall complex at the end of May 1973. It was a change to go there, wasn't it? Something very different.

The ominous presence of the CLDC at Cuerden Hall kept making itself known to us during the mid-months of this year, when locals learned about long lists of land, including many farms and footpath routes etc, which were to be compulsory purchased. This was necessary for sewage pipes, drains, roads and so on to be built, plus many new houses of course. Astley Farm, close to the hall, was one of those to be compulsory purchased, along with all of its land, which stretched from Southport Road to Euxton Lane, abutting Dutch Barn Farm, which stood near to the new hospital entrance at the top of Euxton Lane.

Acquisition of the farm allowed those of us interested in archaeology to 'flag up' to the CLDC the need for an excavation to be carried out when the site became available. This was prompted by the finding of pottery, associated with Bronze Age burials, at the farm in the 1960s. This new dig would search for further evidence at the site.

In June, the Gillibrand Barn Arts Centre was opened, and, even at the outset, there were a great many people saying that the barn was to be a place which would be a bit of a 'closed shop', and unavailable to most people. In retrospect, this probably was the case, for the events at the barn subsequently catered for a minority interest. This was unfortunate, for I recall writing many letters to local and national organisations (on behalf of the local Historical Society), about how we could ensure the future of the building. We put a lot of effort into creating an awareness into the importance of this building. It should still be a building for Chorley people, and should never have become a private residence as it did later. It is one of the town's listed buildings, and one which, with some foresight by the Arts personnel running it, would still be a public building.

Mid-1974 saw the site levelled and work start on the foundations for the new St George's Primary School, at the corner of Carr Lane with Bolton Road. A couple of months later, there was a proposal to build an eight-storey office block at the bottom of Church Brow, which had now become Church Steps. The building would be on the site of the two houses which later became the Swan with Two Necks pub. The office building application to council was refused, but a proviso was included, that the council would be in favour of such a building to be on the site of the old Parish Institute and its bowling green, which extended to Water Street at the back of the building. Another scheme that came out around November, was a plan to build a multi-storey car park in the rear gardens of Chorcliffe House.

In December, the Gillibrand Arts Centre sought to change its name to the Gillibrand Community Centre. Apparently, it had been realised that the original name and the events and activities that took place there were not to the taste of the majority. At this time, it was also said that the Trustees of Gillibrand Barn were in debt.

A particular memory I have for December that year, was of an old film which had come to light and been reprocessed, so that it could be shown on up-to-date equipment. It was a short film taken in Chorley, from around 1913 to the later 1940s. The film was called *Cavalcade of Chorley*, and was shown first to an invited audience, which included myself, due to my involvement with local history. Although the film was not too good as far as its quality went, its content was very interesting. What happened to that archive of Chorley is unknown. Perhaps it should be resurrected and be shown once more.

Here are a few reminders of what we were discussing by the end of 1974. Car parking was becoming more and more of a problem in Chorley, and the multi-storey proposal for Chorcliffe gardens was seen as a partial cure to the problem. Also under discussion was the road on stilts over Chorley 'bottoms', linking Park Road with Bengal Street. What this was supposed to be for is anyone's guess. Shortly after these schemes for Water Street and Hollinshead Street had been mooted, a 'Conservation Area' was established in that area.

The new year of 1975 saw Clayton Hall and Park Hall developments in the news once again. The Clayton Hall site had been refused permission to be developed as a leisure complex. The owners were now concentrating their development on Park Hall and this was where they took much of the stonework so controversially removed from Clayton Hall. With Clayton Hall being a listed building, the removal of stonework should not have taken place, yet the owner was not served an enforcement notice at the time to make good or replace the stonework which had been removed. This was under consideration.

On a personal note, the 1970s was a time of change as far as my employment was concerned. It was a time during which I became involved with three organisations in addition to my role as secretary of the Historical and Archaeological Society. But these activities were not the only ones during this time. Realisation that the many historical buildings in and around Chorley area were in poor condition, despite their so-called protection, led me to carry out a detailed survey of them all. This took up several months. I found that five of those listed buildings had been demolished, three were in very poor condition and many of the others were in need of attention.

The outcome of the survey was a report which was sent to the Planning Department of Chorley Borough Council. I was also interviewed by the *Lancashire Evening Post* and the *Chorley Guardian*, both of which produced extensive coverage of the work I had conducted, along with their own comments on this poor state of affairs regarding those local buildings which were supposed to be protected. As some of them were in the Water Street area, concern about the condition of these older buildings was taken up by a group which was concerned about the number of older cottage properties in and around the Water Street/Parker Street areas. They advocated that many of these old houses need not be demolished, but could be refurbished. This group was headed by Val Feld and Ross Hubbold, who contacted local MP George Rogers to ask for his support, and to preserve rather than demolish.

In February, the Gillibrand Centre closed, by now having debts of some £7,000. During March, the Nat West Bank was refurbished, and the old panelling, including the counters, was sold to a purchaser from the USA.

The environment continued to be the in-thing to talk about and get involved with on a worldwide basis, and this cascaded down to local groups such as those in Chorley. During April, a conference was called in the Town Hall, at which interested groups and organisations presented their views and listened to speakers. As well as presenting a paper regarding my concerns about the historical environment in Chorley, I expressed much concern about Buckshaw Hall and Worden Hall within the ROF at Euxton.

During May, it was announced that the Chorley Sub-Aqua Club had been working on a wrecked ship off the coast of Anglesey. This was a former Royal Yacht which had sunk during the 16th century. However, the talking point in many Chorley homes in June, was the closure of a family shop in Fazackerley Street – a shop which was probably the last in Chorley where butter, taken from a large tub was formed into moulds by patting. This shop, of course, was Dunderdale's. I was fortunate to be able to look around the upstairs rooms of the shop as it was about to close. These rooms had so much in them from years before which would have made good exhibition material, if we had had a heritage centre in Chorley . Both a heritage centre and a museum is something which is long overdue.

In June 1975, work began at the former Odeon to convert the cinema into a bingo hall. It was stated by Coral Bingo, that on completion of the work, their existing premises in the former Tudor dance hall in Gillibrand Street would be closed. The Tudor will be recalled by many readers. After all, it was a special place to many of us. I expect some will recall going to the 'pictures' there as well, for it used to be a cinema called the Hippodrome. Of course, when the Bingo Club at the Tudor was closed, it then became a supermarket. Was it called Graham's? When the supermarket vacated the premises, it was not used again.

Close to the Gillibrand Centre, which had been part of the Home Farm to Gillibrand Hall, an area of land, plus a viaduct over a deep valley, which carried the north carriage drive from the hall, was gifted to the town. Here was surely an opportunity to create a mini-park, with the barn as a centrepiece attraction. However, the barn was sold to become a private residence, the viaduct was demolished and some of the land was used for building more houses, as was to take place adjoining the barn. One stone was saved from that viaduct – a stone which has the crossed swords of the Gillibrand family upon it. It resides near Astley Hall, with no recognition as to its origins or historical association.

Popular newsagent Jack Monks died in July of that year. His wife was Councillor Mrs Connie Monks, who had become an MP in 1970. Mr Monks' later shop was across from the Police Station, next door to the Court Tavern pub. His earlier shop was also next to a pub, a little further along St Thomas's Road, nearer to Market Street. The pub was the Wheatsheaf, now called the George.

That shop was my parents' newsagent, as we lived so close, in Farrington Street, behind the Police Station, where the courthouse stands today. I suppose it was inevitable that sooner or later I would spend some time as a paper lad for Jack Monks. The round delivering those papers extended down St Thomas' Road to Southport Road, and along many of the roads, streets and avenues

off St Thomas' Road. In fact, it was 'my area' – an area that I knew very well.

The Clayton Hall saga was still running on during August. As yet, there had been no move by the owners to rectify the damage caused to the hall by the removal of stonework, which had made it structurally unsound. To counter this, it was propped up with wooden baulks, which were soon removed or set on fire, this time by 'unofficial vandalism'.

Duxbury Park gardens were officially opened to the public during September – the same month that Chorley lost its postmark, for letters posted at the GPO were no longer being sorted at Chorley, but were taken to Preston. The Chorley postmark still continued in use for businesses and council letters, which of course were franked at their premises.

Earlier, I mentioned how the CLDC had been asked to allow an archaeological dig to take place at Astley Hall Farm. The permission for this to start came in September 1975. By this time, the groups who would be involved with the work were ready. These were the local Chorley and District Historical and Archaeological Society and the West Lancashire Archaeological Society. The director of the dig was to be Mr J. Hallam, who was the consultant archaeologist for the CLDC. The dig began with a small excavation, which was photographed by the local papers. The photograph shows Mr Hallam, Mrs J. Lewis of West Lancs Society and myself of the Chorley Society. The start of the dig saw us discovering Bronze Age pottery, as had been found 10 years earlier. We continued the work to see what else we could find. This proved to be the cremated remains of seven people – all female – dating from about 1500BC. It was quite a discovery.

The new Bingo Hall, in the former Odeon, opened in October, with a visit by the mayor. Celebrity guest at the opening was Julie Goodyear *Coronation Street's* Bet Lynch of the Rovers Return pub. A total of 1,100 spectators attended that opening, but I have been unable to obtain any photographs of the event. I'm sure that there must have been plenty taken.

From a general point of view, one of the things which I noted in my journals of the time, was that 1975 seems to have been a year in which the local clubs in the area reached a zenith. Every week in the local media, half a page or more was taken up with advertisements for all those clubs. That is without including the Church Clubs, which often held dances or bingo etc. Think of the names of all those that we had in Chorley in the 1970s.

Do you recall where Whelan's supermarket used to be? It was the first supermarket to be built in the former Haydocks Sawmills in Clifford Street. This building was later taken over by Morrison's. Incidentally, Whelans was opened by television celebrity Stuart Hall.

Environmental issues continued to dominate the headlines at the end of 1975 and into 1976. Many of these were not just relative to the natural environment. It had become more widespread, to discuss recycling of consumable packaging, of glass, paper, tin and aluminium cans and so on. The historical environment was one of my concerns, as it still is today, for if we do nothing about retaining it, what will the next generation have as our legacy to them? Not very much, I think. These issues are as relevant today as they were in 1976.

Regarding Clayton Hall in January 1976, the CLDC and CBC set up a meeting with the local Clayton Parish Council, to discuss the future of the hall. It had now become a liability, and it was even proposed that the hall and site should become the subject of a public inquiry.

Also this month, Civil Engineer Mr Leonard Fairclough died. He had been a leading figure in Civil Engineering worldwide, from his Adlington premises. Mr Fairclough Senior had started the company in 1883. Mr Leonard Fairclough had run the company from 1927 to 1965, when he retired.

The environmental awareness which was such a focal point in the later 1970s, was one of the contributing factors leading to a start being made, during March 1976, on the clearing of years of neglected pathways and open spaces, of trees and shrubs which had taken over, in the so-called Chinese gardens below Rivington Pike, by conservation workers. These gardens were originally private grounds surrounding the bungalow built by Lord Leverhulme on the slopes of the hill. They were a wonder of landscaping, with grottos and waterfalls being created on the steep hillside. The original residence was burned down by a lady of the suffragette movement, and a second bungalow was built of stone.

When Liverpool Corporation took over the Rivington area to provide a water catchment area, the thinking was that only a minimal number of people should visit the beauty spot that is Rivington and its Pike. To discourage visitors to the Bungalow Gardens, to give them their real

name, the bungalow itself was demolished and the gardens allowed to become overgrown – something which, I feel, should never have happened.

In Astley Park during March, an excavation for a new sewage pipe saw a huge amount of environmental damage done between the entrance gate and the boating lake and paddling pool. The new pipe was intended to ensure that no pollution occurred to the River Chor, which flows through the park. Near to Astley Park, at the west end, where the CLDC had compulsorily purchased all the farmland, the new Astley Village was being built. By June, the first rented houses had been officially opened by the chairman of the CLDC, Sir Frank Pearson. A time capsule was buried in the foundations of one of the North British Housing properties.

On 5 July 1976, Clayton Hall was demolished, which caused a storm of protests from not only historians and conservationists, but also from many local people, who were disgusted that this had been allowed to happen to a supposedly listed building, particularly since it had been made unsafe by the removal of supporting stonework by the owners. Nor had those owners been enforced to repair the building by the local authority. The weak excuse for its demolition was 'it was near a public footpath'.

In Chorley we were hearing the first mention of possible pedestrianisation in the town centre in the not-too-distant future, plus improvements to traffic flow. Many trials for traffic flow improvement took place, including an experiment with one-way traffic along Cleveland Street, going south, with traffic going out of Fazackerley Street northbound only, and out of Chapel Street into Market Street going south only.

About this time, the widening of Bengal Street led to the 'three-cornered rec' being made smaller. The adjoining Parish Church Girls' School had been empty for a time, and was converted into the Rose and Thistle Club. A road access was made from Dacca Street, across the rec to the former schoolyard, to allow vehicles to enter from that side. This further reduced the rec – an important local amenity. Adjoining that schoolyard for the girls, were the school allotments for boys from Hollinshead Street School, and I recall we were always in trouble for paying more attention to the girls than to our plots.

My notes and cuttings from the later part of 1976 were not too detailed, but I did record that the Gillibrand Barn Centre had been sold, and that patients at Chorley

Hospital had a show business visitor in the form of singer Anita Harris, who was performing at Park Hall. Also, that more houses had been built in Astley Village, and many of the roads had been given names which were based on the old field names that were on plans of the Astley Farm lands.

The Parish Institute on Park Road was now a horrible eyesore, and was still a 'mecca' for vandals. As it was in such a prominent position across the road from Astley Park, and on the main road through town, many questions and letters were appearing in the local press about what was to be the future of the building.

It had been last used in the 1960s as a Church Institute, with many facilities. Why it became disused is still a question many people ask. It was subsequently used by Chorley College. The building dated from 1905, according to the date stone – which on demolition I obtained, to keep for many years. I gifted it back to the Parish Church when the new institute was built in the 1990s, where it has been built into the wall, adjoining the steps up to the first floor.

We lost a popular sight in late 1976, when it was discovered that the huge laburnum tree, which stood near the west end of Chorley Parish Church, was in poor condition. It already had many of its long branches propped up, and so it was decided by the church authorities that the tree had to be cut down. Thus, we had seen the last of that beautiful sight of yellow flowers.

So we entered into 1977 and the Queen's Silver Jubilee year. It was to be a year which saw the town dressing, as well as celebrating the occasion. The mayor from 1976 into 1977 was Councillor Jim Moorcroft, who did much for the town's Arts Association, and was of course leader of the council as well. We started off the year once again with environmental concerns. This time it was because of the likelihood that the Ellerbeck area was to become an opencast coal mining site. Mr George Birtill was replaced by Mr Graham Johnson as editor of the *Chorley Guardian*, and George was awarded the title of Honorary Historian for Chorley by the mayor, Jim Moorcroft. That title died also, with the loss of George Birtill, who was often my mentor, yet always a colleague in historical matters.

Did any readers manage to get into Lead Mine Valley during February, when Granada Television were filming for the drama play *Hard Times*? The only way you could

actually get to see what was going on, was if you came in from the Jepsons Gate footpath, to approach by the RAF Memorial.

Two houses at the bottom of Church Steps, that were in a poor state of repair, became the focus of attention as the local authority were accused of neglecting them – as had been seen with the Clayton Hall affair, the selling off of the Gillibrand Centre and the demolition of the carriage drive viaduct. As this debate went on, old property in Steeley Lane and Sherbourne Street was demolished.

In April 1977, a selection contest for Chorley's Carnival Queen and Princess took place, being judged by Chorley Carnival Committee. The chosen Queen was Penny Grieveson. The chosen Princess was Colette Woods. Prizes were presented by His Worship the Mayor of Chorley, Councillor Jim Moorcroft. Towards the end of 1977, Chorley's Penny Grieveson won the title of Carnival Queen of Great Britain.

May 1977 was the month when Jim Moorcroft became mayor of the new district. It fell to the mayor, not only to carry out his normal mayoral functions, plus the many separate functions for mayoress, Mrs Margaret Moorcroft, during his year of office, but, as 1976 would be followed by the Queen's Silver Jubilee Year of 1977, also to do much preparation work in advance of his successor. He also officially opened the Duxbury Jubilee Golf Course. Many questions were asked about why the new golf shop, changing rooms, cafeteria and toilets had been built in brick the middle of such a prestigious range of stone buildings.

Also under debate was why the range of former Duxbury Hall buildings adjacent to the new building had not been used for this purpose. It seemed a logical thing to wonder. We had long heard about the historical association of the location with Myles Standish and the project had seemed an ideal way of making use of the old buildings. Quite simply it seems, the old range of buildings, which were part coach house and part employee quarters for the hall, were leased to a company or companies, and, it seems, could not be used for conversion to golfing premises. Of course, this begat more questions as to why such a ridiculous situation had arisen. At the time, someone asked a question about forward planning, with reference to the lease of the old building and why the need to use it was not foreseen, as the plans for the golf course did not appear overnight. Apparently, all the old buildings at Duxbury Hall are leased to companies remote from the local council. Even the 16th-century Cruck Barn is threatened with conversion to office premises. Surely this very special building should have absolute protection from such a proposal. This barn is similar to the inside of Hall Barn (or Top Barn), at Rivington. Although not unique, it is the only such building of such a size in Chorley. Food for thought perhaps.

Towards the end of his mayoral year, in 1977 that is, the mayor planted a tree between the Town Hall and the courthouse, to mark the start of Jubilee Year. All the Parish Councils in Chorley organised similar planting events simultaneously. The tree was planted following the inaugural speech by Prince Charles, to officially open this special year. A plaque was erected to mark the occasion, but is no longer there. What happened to it? Among the mayor's final duties was the opening of the Duxbury Golf Course on 15 May 1977, the day before Mayor Moorcroft stepped down, to be replaced by Councillor Margaret Raby, who would be the Silver Jubilee mayor through 1977 into 1978.

June 1977 was the official month of celebration for the Queen's Silver Jubilee Year. It was celebrated in Chorley with flags and bunting in some areas. There were plenty of flags in evidence, of course. Some 25 years later, flags were flying again, both for the Queen's Golden Jubilee and for England's bid for the World Cup in the Far East.

The Chorley Jubilee Carnival was rather special, yet I have not been able to get many photographs of the procession. The theme of the carnival was anything relevant to the 25 years of Her Majesty Queen Elizabeth's reign. It was quite an event, and despite it raining, there were a good number of spectators lining the streets to watch it pass from Eaves Lane to Park Road, then into Astley Park.

Leading the procession were mounted police, followed by the band of the Royal Scots Dragoon Guards. That was quite a band as well. Then came the procession of floats etc, entered by businesses, parish councils, churches and many other organisations. I'm afraid I don't recall which of the floats won prizes for their efforts, but some of them were excellent, illustrating many events that had taken place since 1952.

Some of those I do recall were the Mawdesley float, depicting the conquest of Mount Everest in 1953, the huge float from Hoghton, which depicted the Queen's visit to Canada in 1957, and the Heapey float showing the 1961 tour of India (that float took six weeks to build). From Euxton was the investiture of Prince Charles at Caernarvon Castle in 1969. That float even had a castle built on the wagon. The time spent building this float was quoted as 450 hours.

There were also the girls on the Whitbread Brewery float, with their mini-skirts. That was a popular float with the male spectators. The Charnock Richard float depicted the Royal Mint. The Scottish and Newcastle Brewery float seemed to have picked a good theme, with their umbrellas to shelter under.

Some of the floats, whilst retaining a royal theme, chose to use historical events rather than the last 25 years. For example, Sacred Heart Church Young Wives had King Henry VIII and his wives. What about that float from the Mayfield Special School – the one that made the Royal Yacht *Britannia* out of a wagon? Quite brilliant. Such a shame that it was raining on the day.

Carnival Queen Penny Grieveson was officially crowned on the field by recording group The Brothers, who were appearing at Park Hall. The Carnival Princess, Colette Woods, was also in attendance at the crowning event. Events in the arena included a free-fall parachute display and the Chorley Pipe Band.

During June many street parties took place in and around the town, and some of them had to be hastily removed to indoor venues due to the rain. Nevertheless, all seemed to have been enjoyed, but – and this is perhaps because it was a bad day – photographs of those parties are few and far between. I think that after the celebrations of June, the rest of 1977 seems to have had a low-profile, but there were some things worthy of mention in brief. For example, work on the opencast coal excavations was started, and Environment Secretary Peter Shore visited the Cowling area in Chorley, where £125,000 was to be spent on redevelopment.

Who saw Conservative leader Margaret Thatcher when she came to Chorley in August? She visited the hospital, and was caught up in the protest that was ongoing, about keeping the A & E Department open. She later visited B & R Taylor's in Lyons Lane, and the Town Hall to meet council leaders.

This photograph was taken in 1977, when future Prime Minister Mrs Margaret Thatcher came to Chorley. Whilst here, Mrs Thatcher visited the hospital where she met with local people campaigning for a 24-hour accident and emergency facility. She also visited B. & R. Taylor's Engineering Works in Lyons Lane and the Town Hall.

Wall graffiti was becoming more widely seen in the country generally, which, I think, was largely influenced by the popularity of American films and television programmes. We were getting small areas of it locally. However, it was still a bit of a shock to see that big wall painting in Friday Street, in late August – this one officially done – depicting a beach scene. Another major change for the town came to light when it was announced that Park Road Methodist Chapel was in a poor state of repair, and applications were to be sought to demolish it. The two houses mentioned previously, at the bottom of Church Brow, which were in a poor condition, were given the possibility of a new lease of life, after it was proposed by John and Chris Hall to convert them into a pub. It was nice to be involved with the historical aspects of the proposed new pub with John and Chris.

On a sad note, those of us who attended Hollinshead Street School in the 1950s were saddened by the report in

a September newspaper that the former headmaster at Hollinshead Street School, Mr Firth, had died aged 63.

By late October 1977, the Ellerbeck Colliery opencast coal working was well under way, now covering a 195 acre site. That same month, the Pavilion Cinema, which had closed in 1973, was in the news again. It had been purchased by a new owner, who was proposing to alter the inside to create dance halls, a cabaret and a small cinema. These proposals sounded quite encouraging. It was hoped to reopen again in 1978. Also in the news this month was the Headless Cross in Anderton, when the upper portion of the stone, forming the cross, was found in Preston.

How many readers were extras in what became known as 'that film'? Remember the sequel to *National Velvet,* this one being named *International Velvet?* It was being shot at at Park Hall. The film appears regularly on television, and each time I always watch it for the Park Hall scenes.

Clayton Hall may have been demolished, but nearby a

historical Cruck Barn remained. This was set on fire during October. The proposed sale of Heskin Hall caused additional concern and the old Parish Institute building was offered to North British Housing Association, for possible conversion to flats.

Another pair of old buildings were demolished in January 1978. These were next to the Parish Church Rectory on Park Road. One of these was a doctor's surgery for some time. Reminders of 1961 returned later that month when, after subsidence on the White Hart car park, the area was excavated to investigate the cause of the problem. It was found to be due to the settling of brick filling in the former cellars of the Red Lion. The cellar walls were once again revealed for a time, before being refilled correctly.

A proposal to create what was called the West Pennines Country Moors Park was mooted in early March. A public meeting was held in Rivington Barn, and I recall that it was well attended. This new park would extend from Lever Park, Rivington, eastward to Haslingden Grane. In general, the audience at the barn were a bit reserved about some of the schemes proposed, but by and large, felt that it was a good idea. In March 1978 a talking newspaper for the blind was established by the Pat Keene Welfare Centre for the Blind in Crown Street. About this time, the Methodist Chapel on Park Road was finally demolished, not even retaining stone walls at the front and sides. Instead, a brick building, without character, was built on the site. Exactly the same thing happened at the Baptist Chapel in St George's Street. The organ from Park Road Chapel went to Texas, USA, I am informed, but the organ in the Baptist Chapel was still in place during demolition, and so was presumably lost.

By August 1978, the new Astley Village was in a well-developed state, with houses, shops and a squash court building on the site of the former archaeological dig of 1975–6 without any recognition of the site's previous historical value. It would be some time later before a stone was placed near the site of the excavation to commemorate the site's significance. The stone was vandalised with paint soon after.

The old property at the top of Byron Street was demolished by early September. This had been a farm many years before, and was latterly used as a printing works. The site was cleared to allow the building of the new Civic Offices, fronting on to Union Street.

September was the month that the shock of the CLDC's plan to build a road through Duxbury Woods, emerging on Wigan Lane, came to light. This was to run from Coppull New Road via Eaves Green. This scheme has gone on for some time now, and is still, at the time of writing, at a 'pending' stage. Latterly, the route has shifted, to emerge on Bolton Road, between the Yarrow Bridge and Duxbury Gate Lodge. It will still destroy much woodland and local amenities if it goes ahead.

Who would have believed that, in the Eaves Green development area, so much good agricultural land would have been swallowed up? Land has been lost at each side of Burgh Lane, even on to the Burgh Hall site itself, and beyond towards Birkacre Lodges and the River Yarrow. Perhaps it will stop when the development reaches Coppull.

In late September, there was a protest march from Carr Lane via Market Street, and on to the hospital, when it was estimated that 7,000 people took part, many carrying placards highlighting the need for a 24-hour casualty department at Chorley Hospital, plus a need for upgrading the hospital in general. It was this campaign which dominated the local media into 1979, but this was soon displaced by the news that four new industrial areas were to be created in Chorley. These were to be at Ackhurst, Chorley North, Hartwood and Shade Lane, Duxbury.

Early in the year we started to hear the new abbreviated term 'GIA', meaning General Improvement Area. It was applied firstly to the Parker Street area, where local residents had got together to try and stop the demolition of old property and to renovate it instead. This Residents' Action Group, run by Ross and Chris Hubbold, stemmed from an earlier group concerned with the older buildings in the area. Not only did the group deal with the local council, it also created many fun events, which were well attended.

I noted in March 1979 an amusing incident regarding the Town Hall that I'm sure you'll all remember. This was when all four faces on the Town Hall clock showed a different time. This fault was soon rectified by Ray Clayton of Riley Green, who still looks after the clock. In fact, I was with him recently in 2002 on a visit to the Town Hall clock and belfry.

In March, there were picket lines outside the ROF at Euxton, due to a pay dispute and in April, the Chorley

During 1976–7, council proposals to demolish terraced property in and adjoining Parker Street led to an action group being formed, chaired by Ross Hubbold, shown here with wife Chris. Subsequently, a 'General Improvement Area' was created, which held many street events.

programme on Chapel Steps, Park Street, followed by the creation of Croston Village Green, working with the Parish Council there. Sadly, at this time, not a lot of people were interested in the preservation of old buildings or improvements to the civic amenities in general, and we got little support. However, we got plenty of press coverage and supplied many reports about our local buildings, liaising closely with Chorley Borough Council Planning Department. In November 1979, demolition work began at Chorley Railway Station, which was built over a century ago. The platform canopies had been shortened in 1965, but this new work would mean total demolition and a full rebuild, except for the level-crossing gatebox. Although many people wondered why

Natural History Society held their first meeting at the Yarrow Bridge pub. I had a shock when, reviewing my notes, I realised that this was so long ago, since I attended that first meeting.

Of course, I took note of Sophia Loren's photograph in our local paper in April 1979, as I'm sure many other fans did as well. It was shown because a Wheelton man had written a song about her, which was played to her by a local radio station in Manchester. The station also arranged for the writer to meet her in Manchester when she was visiting. Lucky man.

A new Civic Society was set up in 1979, after a gap of many years without such an organisation. In the early 1970s, Chorley's first Civic Trust was established, with national affiliations. At that time, I was quite active in that very much hands-on group, at a time when Chorley did not have a Chamber of Trade. We started the restoration

the powers that be chose to keep a level crossing control box, when the gates were never open anyway, which is still the same today. I thought at this time that the 1930s scheme to make Chapel Street go under the railway, where the crossing is now, would have been a very practical thing to do, but it got no further than a proposal. All that was built was a pedestrian subway. That subway should have been extended under the 1990s town centre bypass road, which, although outside the parameters of this book, is relevant, because getting across the road there is still very dangerous, even with a crossing. On the subject of subways, I wonder if we will get a subway from the new bus station, under the bypass road to the railway station, to be open during the daytime only? But that decision lies in the future.

Before I end my notes about the 1970s, I'd just like to mention that the last chapter of the photographic section concerns the Royal Ordnance Factory and many of the people, and some events that occurred, as well as many traditional things which have now gone from that site forever. I hope that this is of interest, in particular the many people we see in those photographs, for I do feel that people like to look at other people. You might see someone you know.

So we arrive at 1980, and just into the new year, the press was saying that 'Chorley's Pride now Turned to Shame'. This shame was the eyesore on Park Road – the formerly very grand Parish Institute. The building was now very dangerous, and a place that 'undesirable' persons had begun to use, and it was also badly vandalised by this time.

This new decade would see many of our former cotton mills demolished or closed. Mills such as Redan, Croft, Cowling Bridge, Mavis and Coppull Ring. All of these had to be measured and photographed – a task which I undertook – and all of this information will be incorporated into an industrial history of Chorley in the future. In addition to all the recording work, I was chair of the Astley Hall Society, secretary of the Historical and Archaeological Society and vice-chair of the Civic Trust in Chorley. The 1980s would be every bit as busy as the 1970s. But it was rewarding to have much success with conservation and preservation work on buildings, etc.

It is not possible to discuss everything that happened during a eventful a decade as the 1970s was, but, perhaps, many memories will have been rekindled by my notes of the time. The photographic chapters in this volume cover many things that I have not previously discussed, such as local pubs, the M61 and so on. All of these will, I hope, serve as reminders to all who read this work – not just those living in Chorley, but also to those now living around the globe. I hope that this latest volume will provide as much enjoyment as previous ones seem to have.

At the end of the previous two chapters – the 1950s and 60s – I gave a brief mention of what we were buying, watching, listening to or wearing. After some discussion with friends, I have compiled a similar list for the 1970s. I hope that this, too, is a source of memories about what you bought and for whom – whether or not you bought, heard or watched any of the following in Chorley or other local towns.

Apart from decimalisation in 1971, joining the

In March 1970, Skelhorn's of Chapel Street, Chorley, still advertised furniture in pounds, shillings and pence. Decimalisation was still a year away.

Common Market in 1973, Watergate in the USA in 1974, Concorde going into service in 1976, or even the Queen's Silver Jubilee Year of 1977, we all have our own special memories of the 1970s. Perhaps yours was a singer or a song. Groups like Abba, The Osmonds, Showaddywaddy, Pink Floyd, or the Bay City Rollers, and singers such as David Bowie, David Cassidy, Kate Bush, David Essex, and Marc Bolan dominated the airwaves in the 1970s and we all had our individual favourite. Or were you fascinated when Rolf Harris showed us all how we should be playing that 'Stylophone' in 1970?

By 1979, of course, we'd become used the just pounds and pence, as this advertisement for Morrisons shows. No Sunday or Bank Holiday opening in those days either. And the Chorley branch closed on Wednesday afternoons.

What films did we go to see (which we've seen many times since on television)? Here are a few 1970s films: Clint Eastwood's *Dirty Harry* or *Magnum Force* of 1974, *The Godfather* (1971), *Jaws* in 1975. Was Roger Moore's Bond in the 1974 *Live and Let Die* one you liked? For many, I'm sure a favourite will be John Travolta in either *Saturday Night Fever* in 1977, or *Grease* in 1978.

On television, we were still watching the soap operas *Coronation Street*, *Crossroads* and *Emmerdale Farm*. But the cops and robbers shows were favourites, like *Starsky and Hutch*, *Charlie's Angels*, *The Sweeney*, *The Avengers* and *The Professionals*. There were those great sitcoms like *Rising Damp*, *Man About the House*, *On the Buses* and *The Good Life*. And who can forget the epic *Upstairs, Downstairs*? For children (and many adults) there was *Dr Who*, *Bagpuss*, *Catweazle* and *Star Trek*. But what 'did it' for me was *The Muppet Show*. Now that's one show that should have a re-run or a new series. Toys like Klackers, skateboards and the 'Chopper' bike were popular. Fashionwise, hot pants were popular with both sexes – for the girls to wear and the boys to look at. Platform shoes and flared trousers were common with both sexes. Punk was in, then skinhead styles took over.

All of these recollections, spanning some 30 years or so – whether they were about a song, a singer, a film, or an event in Chorley or one of its villages – were all part of our social history, and all of us were participants in one way or another. Having compiled this work from notes and cuttings of the time, I believe a certain piece of text is applicable now. That text comes from the Bible in the Chapter of St John. It simply says 'Gather up the pieces, that none shall be lost'. I have tried to do just that, to rekindle memories that may have been forgotten.

STREET SCENES
PALL MALL TO UNION STREET

Our street scenes around Chorley begin with this view, taken at the Pall Mall, Moor Road junction with Weldbank Lane and Tootell Street. The year is about 1965, and as yet, there are no traffic lights at the very busy crossroads. Imagine if that was still the case today!

A little further down Pall Mall is the junction with Duke Street. In our picture, taken at the end of the street, girls from Duke Street School, where they have attended a cookery lesson, cross Pall Mall. Note the cobbles, and the property on the corner as it was in 1955.

Looking back to Duke Street corner again, notice the property beyond the corner, now having been replaced. The cobbles are covered in this photograph of 1966.

Viewed in the opposite direction to the previous photograph, also in 1966, we look towards St George's Church in the distance, beyond Pall Mall junction with Market Street. Some changes have taken place since then, with buildings to the right demolished.

A memory-jerker for you now! This view looks across the newly created car park towards the Eagle and Child pub in the mid-1960s. To the right, the buildings of St George's School and Institute. But what was the name of the street that the photograph was taken from?

Nearing the end of Pall Mall about 1970, St George's Institute to the right. At the end of Fleet Street to the left, is a sign telling us all to prepare for the coming of decimal currency, with values of all the new coins given on the poster.

Looking back into Pall Mall from the Market Street junction, to the left St George's School extension with Institute beyond. Note the barber's shop, with pole, to the right. This was just in Fleet Street. Photograph taken early 1970s.

In Fleet Street now, and a view past the corner of Gillibrand Walks to the left. The old houses of Fleet Street are in the process of being demolished in early 1962. Note the Pavilion cinema poster to the left.

Cheapside is between Fleet Street and Market Street with the old weavers' cottages next to Owen's Garage. Across Market Street is the shop Poppycock. The houses to the right are gone. A garden area has been created here in 2002, and a replacement 'ancient' cross erected.

Another view along Fleet Street and across Pall Mall to the former St George's Institute. Cheapside is to the left. The corner house used to be a pub many years ago. The end of Gillibrand Walks can be seen to the right. This used to be a lane leading to Gillibrand Hall.

Also off Fleet Street was Moor Street. All trace of this has gone now, as it forms a part of a car park. This photograph from the later 1960s shows how the street led to a set of gates leading into Primrose Cottage, also visible in the photograph.

Moving into Devonshire Road now, this view is close to the end of Carrington Road, looking towards Coronation Rec. Visible are the Barracks and the former Devonshire Road Wine Stores. The confectioner's shop to the right is now a dispensary. Notice that the road is still cobbled in this photograph dating from the late 1950s.

Another view in Devonshire Road in the early 1970s, with St Mary's Hall to the right, and the school just beyond, with children on their playtime looking over the railings. In the distance is the former Sumner's Corn Mill.

Off Devonshire Road is Peter Street. At the junction of the roads were these large hoardings in the late 1950s, with adverts typical of the time. To the extreme right is a poster advertising a 'Brains Trust' in the Town Hall.

Off Peter Street is Dole Lane, which used to be part of the old footpath system from Town Green, the former Town Hall Square, which ran towards the Gillibrand area. In our late 1960s view, the new courthouse is nearly finished, and the old shops are still at the end of the lane.

This is what the old Town Hall Square used to look like before demolition. It's a view taken in 1960 or so, showing newly-painted parking spaces to reduce the number of cars being parked in the square. The old Police Station with Court above is to the left.

In this 1965 view along St Thomas's Road, the old Police Station site and adjoining property had been cleared. Old property still stands in Mealhouse Lane, with the White Hart roof showing above.

In Mealhouse Lane now, looking back to the square and the old Police Station. The date is March 1957, and the reason for the television transmitter vans being here was that a Boxing Competition was under way in the Town Hall. It was the first TV broadcast from Chorley.

Near to the same location as the previous photograph, Mealhouse Lane, this time taken from the Market Street end, with the Red Lion pub to the right. Just past the pub was the former Public Hall (Chorley's first 'moving picture' house), later a British Legion club. The Red Lion was demolished in the early 1960s.

Across Market Street from Mealhouse Lane was the original Union Street, which formed a crossroads. The later Union Street was closer to the Parish Church. Here we see a queue of traffic in 1960, possibly all waiting for petrol at Hughlock Hindle's garage further along the street.

Off Union Street is Fellery Street, and in this early 1970 view, the large house to the left, which dated back to the 18th century, still stands. The houses in the distance stand in Hollinshead Street. To the right, a premises which was Brimley's leather works, now a printers.

In the same location as the previous picture, with Fellery Street to the left, and the old house front now visible. On the foundations of this old house, a modern bungalow now stands, but the steps remain. To the right are huts used by Chorley Teacher Training College.

In the top photograph, taken in Union Street, we look east towards the junction with Clifford Street. The narrowness of Union Street here caused several accidents, leading to the road being made wider by almost the same amount as the original carriageway. The swimming baths are to the right. The bottom photograph looks back along Union Street toward Market Street where the road-widening improvement work can be seen. To the right is the former garage of Messrs Hughlock & Hindle, now the site of the Civic Offices. This work was being done

Chorley's first bus station lasted into the early 1960s, when an improved station was needed. In this view, we see work for the new (and present-day) bus station under way. At the top of the photograph is the Flat Iron market, with refreshment bar. At the time of writing this new station is soon to be replaced and re-sited close to the railway station.

Another view of the Flat Iron marketplace, this time without the market association. The photograph dates from May 1957, when a troupe of aerial high-wire performers visited the town. In the distance are houses in Clifford Street, with the Chortex Mill in the distance.

Adjoining the bus station is the Post Office, which in 1965 was having extensions added at its east and west sides. Here at the west end, in New Market Street, we see work under way on one extension. To the right, the new bus station is now finished.

To the west end of the Post Office, the original ground-floor building was getting an extra two storeys. In this view of January 1966, work is at the new first-floor level, with another storey to build yet, as can be seen in the photograph following, 'View down High Street' (bottom, right).

Back to December 1956 with this view of High Street. Note the still cobbled roads and wide footpath in High Street. The cars give away the date of the photograph. Compare this view with the next photograph.

Another view similar to the last, looking into High Street, this time with a wider view of the back of the Royal Oak, with its car park to the rear, and later cars. The date here is about 1973. A modern-day view, with shops built on the former car park would make a fascinating comparison.

View down High Street towards the Post Office. Here one can see the completed two-storey addition to the original ground-floor building. In the distance the former, recently-built, gas show rooms can be seen. The photograph dates from about 1974.

MAIN STREET TRUNK ROAD

The main road through Chorley was well established in the 17th century. By the 20th century, it had become one of the main north-south trunk routes for all types of vehicles. By the 1960s the traffic was excessive through the town. This view shows the northern boundary into Chorley, at the Sea View pub, and was taken about mid-1960s.

A little nearer to the town, this sweeping bend used to have a significant landmark, visible on the left. It was a water gravity tank, which used to be necessary to pressurise the town's mains water. It had been redundant for some years, and was demolished in 2000.

Running down into Chorley from the north again, this 1960s view looks from the old entrance to the hospital past Hartwood Hall, to the distant bend, shown in the last photograph.

The road through Chorley was a part of the Turnpike Road System from the early 19th century. The north turnpike gate was located close to Chorley Hall, near these cottages. Chorley's Comet store now occupies the site. The cottages were called, appropriately, Turnpike Cottages. Photograph from 1962.

The old route through the town followed Water Street. It was only in 1822 that Park Road was built, and the road diverted. Here in Park Road the wide trunk road is less busy in 1975.

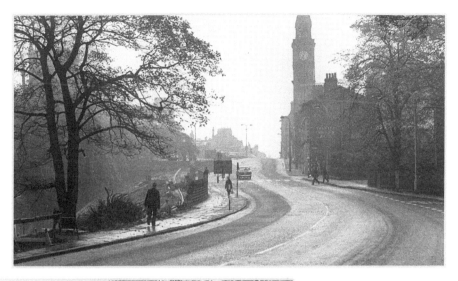

The main road enters the town centre at the park gates bend. By the 1960s it had become a hazard area, with excessive traffic both ways. It thus became necessary to widen the road. To the left, the former Church Brow is being filled in during 1964, to allow the widening to take place.

Looking in the opposite direction from the previous photograph, and a few years earlier, to 1953 in fact. Here we see Park Road to the left, with Church Brow in the centre (the old main road) going downhill to Water Street, along which the River Chor used to flow. To the right is Chorley Parish Church.

Taken in early December 1957, this view looks up Chorley's main street, Market Street, from the end of Fazackerley Street past Woolworth's store, past the tall building in the centre which was the Royal cinema.

From the archway at the bottom of Mount Pleasant, opposite Chapel Street, the view is a little different than today. To the right, the Waterloo pub, and at the end of Fazackerley Street, the large Co-op building. The photograph was taken in 1957. Note the cobbled street surface.

Looking south up Market Street this time from the front of Woolworth's store. The date of the photograph is June 1970, and traffic in the street is typical of the time – busy yet not heavy.

At the corner of Chapel Street/Market Street was a three-storey building which was Stringfellow's shop. By late 1955 the building was being demolished, which seems to have been a hands-on job, with an absence of machines (see next two photographs also for other views).

Viewed from the front of Woolworth's, looking to Chapel Street in 1959, and a temporary shop has been built for Messrs Stringfellow's, Florists. The policeman on duty was once a common sight in Market Street. Note how the street narrows here, at the spot once called the 'Market Street Bulge'.

The same location as the previous two photographs, this time taken in the early 1970s. The infamous 'Bulge' has been removed by demolishing the protruding shops. Messrs Stringfellow's shop now has a first floor, and has been realigned to give a wider street.

Looking down Market Street towards the Town Hall from in front of the Royal, which is to the left. At the bottom of Gillibrand Street is a pub called the Wellington, demolished three years ago. Rebuilding commenced on this site in mid-2002.

By early 1974, there was a new roundabout, viewed here from Bolton Street looking down Market Street. To the left, the former shops have been demolished and cleared (see later chapter on Shops).

Still in Bolton Street, near to the junction with Lyons Lane, we look back into town, to the north. This view was taken in June 1974 at 8.50am and the street is free of traffic. The houses on the left are gone, and have been replaced by the Kwik Save store.

Looking the other way to the previous photograph, we look towards the Duke Street junction. Again the houses to the right are gone, and the whole of this area has been changed with the building of the town centre bypass road, which follows the line of Lyons Lane to the left.

Once again we are looking at the Duke Street crossroads, this time in 1958, when there were, as yet, no traffic lights, but there are five pubs visible. No wonder it was a favourite place to watch traffic then! This is why the term 'up Duke' originated.

I have included this view of the Lyons Lane/Duke Street with Bolton Street junction for it is a scene that has now gone, due to the new bypass road. It will be remembered by most readers, for it was such a busy junction.

To the south side of the Duke Street crossroads, the main road now becomes Bolton Road – still the A6 Trunk – heading towards Manchester. To the left is the end of King Street, with the White Bear pub on the corner.

In the previous photograph, we can just see the front of the former Plaza cinema, which by the 1970s had become a multiplex as they were called, with two screens, later four, to become Studio Four. The cinema closed in the 1980s, but the building survives in 2002.

A view down Bolton Road taken in early 1956, with a total absence of traffic, except one handcart. To the left is the wall and gates into Yarrow House, now the site of Albany High School. The River Yarrow bridge is at the bottom of the hill.

Taken in 1972, the photograph was taken whilst standing on the bridge over the River Yarrow, looking back towards Chorley. As yet no development has started here. The new Carr Lane realignment road has been made, where today St George's School is built.

Street Scenes
Fazackerley Street to Harpers Lane

A view from Cleveland Street to Market Street via Fazackerley Street in 1974. The street had now been pedestrianised as part of a larger scheme that was in the pipeline. The circular seats in the middle of the street soon got the nickname of 'flying saucers'.

This time we look from the Market Street end of Fazackerley Street towards Cleveland Street and the market. In the distance are the buildings in New Market Street, with popular pub, the Fazackerley Arms, to centre right, demolished in the 1990s for a new shopping mall.

Viewed across Market Street towards the Woolworth's store in 1976. Adjoining was the former stone-built District Bank, just demolished to make way for a NatWest bank. Crossing the street with white coat is Mrs Ditchfield, whose husband kept the shoe shop in Chapel Street.

Chapel Street, viewed from the arch at the bottom of Mount Pleasant, leading to St Mary's Church. Note how the traffic is turning left out of the street to go south only. This was part of the one-way system that was in operation in the early 1970s.

October 1965, and this is Clifford Street, looking towards Chapel Street, with St George's Church in the distance. To the left are the curing sheds of Messrs Haydock's Timber Merchants. The works is the building with the tower. To the right, Livesey Street, now demolished.

The railway coal yard is shown here, with coal bags being filled directly from the railway wagons. One of the vehicles being loaded has the side logo of National Coal Board. The big house to the left was in Stump Lane close to the railway bridge. Photograph *c.*1957.

The tower in Clifford Street. This was the works of Messrs Haydock's, where great logs were cut up into planking etc. The works, which ran down one side of Hill Street, adjoining the tower, later became a supermarket.

This is Railway Street in the early 1970s, looking back to Chapel Street. To the right is the railway goods warehouse, with large sidings at the other side where rail wagons were loaded/unloaded. Today in this location is an embankment, blocking the street at its south end, as part of the town centre bypass road.

A regular user of the goods yard were local firm T. Witter, who made lightweight linoleum, sending it to customers and mail order houses by rail. Here tubes of 'lino' are loaded into rail vans, having been brought by horse and cart from Fosterfield/Lower Healey works. Photograph about 1960.

Still looking at the former goods yard on Railway Street, this view was taken from Lyons Lane bridge, and shows the yard in about 1960. One track ran from the yard, to the left, crossing Railway Street, to the railway wagon works. Chorley station is to the right.

By the 1970s, this was the scene from Lyons Lane bridge. Compare it with the previous view. The large shed in centre distance, in front of the station, was built to accommodate T. Witter's 'lino' trade. This shed was later used by Messrs Stewart Longton Caravans.

Speaking of Chorley railway station, this is a view of the station before the canopy was removed in the 1970s. Who was it that said that the station looked 'untidy' with the canopy? The platform we are looking at is that for trains to Preston and the north.

Another 1970s view at the top of Chapel Street, looking towards the station, level-crossing and subway. To the right is Railway Street. Now the new town centre bypass runs left to right across this location, and within a few feet of the subway end nearest to camera.

A rare view of the level-crossing gates at Chorley station open, looking towards Steeley Lane. To the left across the tracks is a former 19th-century foundry. To the right, the white building is a pub with the very obvious name of the Railway.

Into Steeley Lane with this view dating from about 1975. This was a time when there were shops on both sides of the street, and it was busier than it is today. In the distance, Seymour Street to the left, and to the right Little Steeley Lane, with the Regent cycle shop on the corner.

Looking back down Steeley Lane from the corner of Little Steeley Lane as it used to be. Even that name has gone now! In the distance the railway crossing and Chapel Street. This too is a mid-1970s photograph.

At the south end of Little Steeley Lane is Lyons Lane. This view shows the corner of that junction. The buildings to the right were the main offices and a shop for the Chorley Co-operative Society. To the left, those shops are now gone, and the White Lion pub is now a mosque.

Combining two streets we have looked at, now viewed from the end of Brooke Street, looking over Lyons Lane to the Railway Street goods depot in 1972. To the right is the railway bridge in Lyons Lane. Today this view would be looking along the new town centre bypass road.

Lyons Lane ends at Bolton Street, at the crossroads, shown here in about 1974. This road end is now changed, and covered by shrubs and a grassed area. All the property has gone, on both sides of the road, to allow the town centre bypass road to swing in from the left.

Returning back up Lyons Lane, to pass the end of Little Steeley Lane once again. Still in the mid-1970s, we look up the lane towards Eaves Lane, just visible in the distance. To the left, the offices of Messrs B. and R. Taylor's. To the right, the offices of Messrs Lawrences.

Lyons Lane joins Eaves Lane. Here you can turn north towards Botany and Blackburn Road, or south towards Limbrick and Rivington. The latter route is shown here, above Cowling Bridge, with the old mill to the right and cottages to the left, all demolished. Photograph about 1958.

On Eaves Lane again, and a view along the lane from Stump Lane towards Harpers Lane during the late 1970s. Fosterfield Mill can be seen to the right of the photograph, now demolished and built over. It is now the location of Fosterfield Day Centre.

A mid-1950s view now, at the end of Eaves Lane and its junction with Harpers Lane/Botany Brow. To the left is the Hygienic Laundry. To the right, the former 19th-century weavers' cottages. Children from the local school are being escorted across the Harpers Lane crossing.

Harpers Lane, and the Chorley to Blackburn railway passed over the road here. This view shows the line while still in use in about 1965. It was a favourite line for walkers, who caught the train to Heapey Station then walked back to Chorley.

Bengal Street joined Water Street at this corner, by the three-cornered rec, or at the Parish Church girls' school to the right. On the left, Astley Street and old property by the Parish Church boys' school. Some of this property here dated back to the early 1800s.

From the same corner as the previous photograph, here we look down to Chorley Bottoms, as Water Street is called here. This, remember, was the old turnpike road through Chorley. To the right is Garden Terrace, and at the bottom of the hill the old gas works buildings.

Down Botany to Blackburn Road, where the road is carried over the Wigan-Chorley-Blackburn railway line by the bridge in the photograph. The date is August 1957, and a crash had taken place on the line, caused by runaway wagons.

In this photograph, dating from 1965, those gas works buildings are seen at close quarters. They were closed and boarded up at this time, but would be revamped and utilised as an annexe of Chorley College during the 1970s.

Back in Bengal Street, and the bend by the three-cornered rec sweeps to the left, while straight ahead is Dacca Street. On the left is the former Parish Church girls' school. The wide Bengal Street now forms the town centre bypass road. Photograph from the mid-1970s.

In Parker Street, we look across the Astley Street crossroads past the Parish Church boys' school to Commercial Road in the distance. The houses at each side of Parker Street to the left and the right have been demolished. The white building to the right was once a pub.

Still in Parker Street, a street which saw great activity and community spirit in the 1970s, such as a busy action group, getting the area made into a GIA (General Improvement Area). This picture, of about 1960, shows buildings in the middle of the street, at the west side.

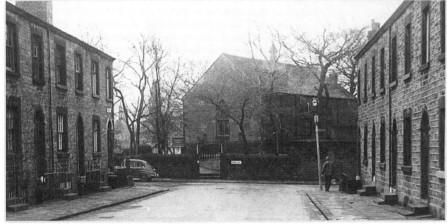

At the bottom end of Parker Street, it joins Park Street, with Park Street Unitarian Chapel directly opposite, as shown here in this early 1960s view. On the left, former handloom weavers' cottages, now restored and listed. Those cottages to the right are now demolished.

Passing out of Park Street on to Park Road, we can return to the town centre. When this photograph was taken in the mid-1970s, we could see this view, opposite the park gates, looking down into Water Street. The former gas works buildings are now being used by Chorley College. To the right, the old Swan Inn.

Remember These Shops?

This was the view you saw from Union Street in the early 1960s. To the right was the Conservative Club, with an alleyway next to it (through which I walked en route to school daily). Next was Tom Wilson's shoe shop then a sweet shop, next was Stones' Grocers. The bike is one I rode for a time doing deliveries for the shop. To the left, the Red Lion pub.

In Clifford Street now, with the corner into Union Street to the left, as it was in the early 1960s – a few years after Union Street had been widened. To the right are houses in Clifford Street, demolished before the town centre bypass road was built. The corner café was also demolished.

Into Market Street now, and shops opposite Fazackerley Street. They were empty in 1962, prior to redevelopment of the three into one unit. The three are Playfair, Griffiths and Telehire.

Fazackerley Street now, with traffic flow experiment under way, in the early 1970s. The shops to the left are; Co-op, Hunton's stationers, Fisher's Carpets, Harry Miller men's shop, Philips' household and stationery. Finally there was Boot's chemist.

Still in Market Street, between Fazackerley Street to the left, and Chapel Street off to the right. Next to Wilcock's corner shop was The Chocolate Shop. Next was Halton's, known as the 'Catholic Repository', plus seven more shops and a pub, from here to Chapel Street corner.

Right: Not really a shopper's view of Chapel Street shops, but a view that is different! It was taken in 1955 from the top of St Mary's Church tower looking up that street, across the railway and into Seymour Street. Note the dome of Miller's building in New Market Street.

From Chapel Street, we look across the road to Woolworth's store, always a 'Mecca', always warm and worth a browse. Why it was relocated we will never know! To the right, as mentioned earlier, the old District Bank with its impressive stone frontage. Photograph taken in June 1960.

Here are two shops viewed in 1961. They were in Cleveland Street. We can see one is Gertrude Wilson's, but what was the other one? I'm sure someone will be able to say.

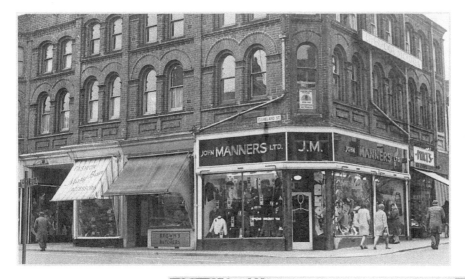

The Victoria Building dating from the 1890s, is viewed here from Chapel Street, with Cleveland Street to the left. The shop names will bring back a few memories, I'm sure. Pity we lost the arcade though! It was a building with many amenities, such as shops, offices and a dance hall.

Looking along Cleveland Street, with the Victoria Building to the right and shops such as John Manners, Brown's butchers, Mary Banks and Sharples'. To the left were Clarkson's and the Maypole. Photograph taken in about 1962.

Sharples' shop was on the Market Place corner, shown here in the 1960s. Remember the motto they had? It said; 'If it comes from a loom, try Sharples first'. Just inside the arcade was the bookshop of Adam Barnes, just visible in the photograph.

Looking through the arcade, with the Health Food Shop to the right. Down steps to the right, is the hairdressing salon of Mr Darlington. From here you looked up to a glass block ceiling, to see people walking overhead. Strange that, while many other big towns in the area have been creating arcades, we had ours demolished!

Further along Cleveland Street near the junction with High Street, and taken a little later than the previous few photographs, in about 1976. To the left, the Market Tavern pub with a health food shop and a solid fuel fires shop. Opposite was the Gayfair, a bookmaker's, a sweet shop and a wig shop.

In Chapel Street, now looking down towards Market Street in the early 1970s. Many of the shops shown here have been rebuilt since the photograph was taken, but many will be remembered, I'm sure, especially those such as Thornley's and Ball and Son's gardening shop.

Further up Chapel Street, more of the shops can be seen on the south side of the street. Do you recall Skelhorn's in the old chapel? How about that Wimpy bar?

Off Chapel Street is New Market Street. In this view some of the well-known shops of the 1970s can be seen, like Millers', Tom Higham's and Relayvision.

Taken at the same time as the previous picture, in 1975, this view looks up Chapel Street. Here Sharples' shop has relocated to yet another corner plot, formerly the Victoria pub, usually referred to as the 'horsebox'. This site is now occupied by Dixons.

In Steeley Lane perhaps the best known shop, where many of us got our first bicycle in the 1950s or '60s, was the Regent Cycle Store, which is the white shop in the middle distance. Another well-known shop here was the Bevan Herb Shop, which was interesting to visit.

Nowadays, this north side of Steeley Lane has not got as many shops as it had in the early 1970s when the photograph was taken. It is an area which, although supposedly to be improved, never seems to get altered. Surely it's not a case of wrong side of the tracks, is it?

I mentioned the so-called Market Street 'bulge' earlier – here is a closer view of it. As well as being able to see the shops that were there. Next to Stringfellow's at the end of Chapel Street, were Blower's, Gray's, Greenhalgh's, and Christie's café. Photograph from the early 1950s.

We lost the point duty policeman from the middle of Market Street, when he was replaced by a Belisha crossing. In March 1958, people using the crossing were monitored by accident prevention personnel. In the background, Miller's Butchers with Leslie's next door.

A similar location to the previous photograph now, but moving forward to the mid-1970s. The 'bulge' has been straightened, and Miller's has become the International store, advertising 'Double Green Shield Stamps'. Booth's is rebuilt, with Mangnall's next door.

Next to the Mangnall's shoe shop (which had moved from across the road to Woolworth's), was Coombe's shoe repairs, then the large DER TV rental shop on the corner. This was 1974–5. The queue is for the town circular bus, with Mrs Audrey Smith and daughters boarding it.

I referred to these shops in Chapter Two, after demolition. They are, of course, at the corner of Market Street with Pall Mall, here viewed through a procession. From Barton's on the corner, to Bibby's at Cheapside corner, were O'Dell's, Baker's and Booth's. Photograph 1954.

Just into Pall Mall now, looking past the 'Big Lamp' junction around the mid-1950s. The old lamp sadly gone (which could have been electrified), Dickinson's take up three frontages, with Swarbrick's butchers, a second-hand shop, the White Bull and Howarth's snack bar.

Another view of the same junction, with shops in the background, as taken from inside the school garden. A new 'Big Lamp' has recently been erected, with a small island. In the distance, Market Street stretches to the north.

Another view out of Pall Mall looking towards Dickinson's which, by this time, had occupied another premises to the left, giving them four frontages by the mid-1960s when this view was obtained. To the right is Wooley's toy shop, in Bolton Street.

The same 'Big Lamp' junction, looking down Market Street. The shops to the left are gone by now – the later 1970s. A mini roundabout is under construction, and Wooley's toy shop is now Boydell's.

In Pall Mall, near Harrison Road junction, this row of seven shops, with their odd single-storey shop premises, are substantially still the same in 2002, although some improvements have taken place. The photograph dates from the mid 1960s.

The last photograph in this chapter is one taken in Bolton Road, and taken about the same date as the previous photograph, during the late 1950s when the property was being cleared. The Bolton Street Co-op shop was at the end of Queen Street East.

CHURCHES AND SCHOOLS

One of the very many church organised events in Chorley – this photograph was taken at a Boy Scout Association dance during the 1950s. Some of my contemporaries are pictured, such as Eric Barker and Michael Ternant.

To the Town Hall now, and in 1955 an exhibition encompassing church organisations was held. In this photograph, we look at a Girl Guides organisation stall.

Still at the exhibition, and this time we are at the Church Lads' Brigade stall which is highlighting the benefits of joining the organisation.

The building of more council estates in Chorley in the 1950s led to a need for a new church off Moor Road. This was to be called St Anselm's, shown here on the event of the first wedding held in the church, during November 1955.

During 1956, the bells of St Laurence's Parish Church were in need of an overhaul, and were removed from the tower. Four of the bells are seen here prior to removal to the bell founders. I had been a ringer here for some time, but was working at sea when the bells were removed.

The Boy Scout Association had many troops in Chorley and district churches in the 1950s and '60s. Sadly these have declined, as have the CLB groups as well. Here we see the presentation of 'Queen's Scout' badges to members for their achievements in March 1957.

The return of the Parish Church bells after recasting saw this photograph being taken of ringers, such as Jack Gartside, Arthur Rigby, Keith Morris, Geoff Astin, Gerald Wilson, John Kerfoot and others. Sadly, I missed out on being on the photograph again. I was in Calcutta at the time!

By the mid-1950s, All Saints' Mission off Moor Road had become inadequate to cope with more people now living in the area, and funds were raised to build a church. In March 1957, the official stone-laying ceremony was carried out by Mr Leonard Fairclough.

St George's Church had seen major refurbishment during the latter half of 1957. This refurbishment work went on until December, when, after internal redecoration (as in the photograph), the church was reopened by the Rt Revd Baddeley, Bishop of Blackburn.

St George's Church CLB group created a pipe band that went on to play at the World CLB parade at Buckingham Palace, London, and were inspected by HM the Queen. The photograph shows the members of the band who played there in July 1957.

A year after the foundation stone had been laid at All Saints' Church, the building was completed. In late March 1958, the new church was consecrated and opened by the Bishop of Blackburn, Rt Revd W. Baddeley, and Bishop of Burnley, Rt Revd G. Holderness.

The interior of St Laurence's Parish Church, as it was in the 1970s, is shown in both of these photographs. All of the internal layout was altered in the 1990s. The top view looks from the east end of the nave to the bell-ringing chamber in the tower at the west end. In the bottom picture, we look from the south-west door towards the nave and chancel. To the right is the Charnock family pew.

The Parish Church of St Laurence had a fine Institute, opened in 1905. It became uneconomic, and was leased to Chorley College in the '70s, after which it fell prey to vandals and was later demolished. The foundation stone was obtained by the author, who gave it back to the church in the late 1990s, where it has been built into the wall of the new Church Rooms.

In Harpers Lane outside St Peter's Church in April 1967. I am told that it shows a parade saluting a flag, which is about to be 'laid up' in commemoration of CLB's Major 'Ted' Ikin, Company Commander of St Peter's Unit, who had been involved with the local CLB for some 30 years until his death.

A small chapel of which little seems to be known, was this in Hill Street, which became a furniture shop, as seen in our photograph taken in the 1960s.

St George's Street Chapel, as it was in the early 1970s. It was latterly a Baptist Chapel. It has been demolished and rebuilt in brick, instead of retaining the original stone walls reduced to single-storey height, for it is in a conservation area.

Those who were at local schools in the 1950s may remember how we had lessons about road safety, by a visiting Police Constable, whose name I believe was Doland or Dowland. He told stories, and had puppets to illustrate points he raised. His talks were always very popular with schoolchildren at the time.

Another of the town's stone chapels, which was also demolished in the late 1970s, was Park Road Methodist. Here sadly, the building suffered from dry rot problems. Here too, the stonework could have been retained, and the necessary repair work carried out, thus preserving its character.

The owner of this photograph was uncertain when or why it was taken, but he thought it was mid-1950s. I think it may be St George's old school, for I recognise Adam Barnes, Jimmy Tootell and my cousin Ronald Clayton, who went to St George's. Looks like tea is ready!

Taken at Southland School, the photograph shows Sir David Eccles, Minister of Education, who was at the school to perform the official opening at the end of April 1956. Next to Sir David is Headmaster, Mr Townsend. Taken on his tour of the school, the Minister signs autographs.

Thought to be of pupils of Chorley Grammar School, the photograph was taken in the Town Hall in the later 1950s, I am told. As to what is going on, the owner is unaware. It could be some sort of awards presentation I suppose, but that is purely a guess.

Another stone-laying ceremony is under way here. This time the stone being laid is at the new St Alban's School in October 1958. Once again it is Mr Leonard Fairclough laying the stone, attended by local church clergy.

Yet another school was nearing completion during November 1960. This was to be the replacement Grammar School in Southport Road. The existing school in Union Street had become too small. Here the first intake of pupils arrive at the as-yet unfinished school.

This photograph was taken at Southlands also, and shows a group of pupils taking part in a performance of *The Wizard of Oz*. Some of the costumes are quite original, and will probably be a talking point when published!

Taken in March 1965, I am told that this is taken at a local school, but at which one is not known. The young ladies appear to be in night attire. Many are holding dolls or teddies. Perhaps it's a 'going to bed' party or a modelling group, who knows! Somebody will, I'm sure.

The Parish Church used to have two schools, a boys' and a girls', off Water Street. By the late '60s, they had become inadequate and were superseded with a new school off Park Road. In the photograph, the children are seen on the way to their new school in April 1969.

Another Southlands photograph now. This time we seem to be looking at some of the attendees at a fair of some sort. It was taken in the mid-1960s I am told, but have no other information.

St George's School stood at the corner of Pall Mall with Bolton Street. The school was extended with a two-storey block, as shown here, with the Institute beyond the extension.

Most photographs showing the front of St George's Primary School show the whole of the frontage. I thought I would show a different aspect of the school this time. Here we see the remaining frontage of the school, being demolished along with the extension and Institute in 1981.

Hollinshead Street School, shown from the Byron Street side. The original school was the white two-storey building, with a later extension. The open area was formerly Hughlock & Hindle's garage, now site of the Civic Offices building in Union Street. Photographed in the late 1970s.

The Parish Church girls' school in Water Street adjoined the three-cornered rec. After the school was vacated in 1970, it was empty for a time, to become the Rose and Thistle Club, then British Legion. It was demolished in 2000. This view is from Dacca Street in 1976 or so.

CORONATION AND SILVER JUBILEE YEARS

Walking Day in 1953 was rather more special than usual, as it was Coronation Year. The streets were decorated with bunting and flags. Here, children from St Peter's Church lead the procession through Market Street. The girls carrying the 'E II R' banner are Anne Simmonds, Anne Whittam and Pauline Kitching. The girls at each end wore dresses of royal blue, and white net, trimmed with gold bows. The centre girl wore a white dress. All wore gold tiaras.

Many local mills were decorated for the Coronation celebration. In this view, taken in the weaving shed of Diamond Mill in Corporation Street, some of the weavers pose amid the decorated columns and looms.

Another Chorley mill which decorated its weaving shed was the Greenfield Mill off Steeley Lane. It was also known as the Co-op Mill. Here again, some of the employees pose amid the decoration of the shed in June 1953.

At the Royal Ordnance Factory, a sewing shop had been established during the 1940s. That shop produced uniforms etc. in peacetime. Here, we see the shop decorated in celebration of the Queen's Coronation in June 1953. The shop continued working until the 1960s.

At the Royal Ordnance Factory railway station, a large banner was erected on one of the platforms in 1953, which stated 'Loyal Greeting – ROF Chorley'. This banner would be seen by passengers on all the trains passing through the station between Chorley and Leyland.

It is uncertain whether these next three photographs were taken at the same school or not. The first shows Mayor Edith Edwards (1953–4), with infants at a local (unknown) school, before presenting Coronation mugs. The children's poses and footwear are certainly varied!

Inside school now, Mayor Edith Edwards is in the process of presenting those special Coronation mugs, and seems to be posing for the photograph with three sets of twins. Again the school is uncertain.

In this photograph, the mayor appears to be with the older pupils of the school, and is being given a bouquet of flowers after presenting Coronation mugs.

Many street parties of 1953 were abandoned due to rain. Often, any large room was used to set up a table and benches for the party tea. This street party was for residents of Avondale and Westminster Road. It had to be held in a nearby workshop.

Here too, we see another local group of some 50 or so children, at their Coronation party. The owner suggests that it was probably at a local school, and not just a street party. The photograph is interesting, despite having very little information about it.

Taken at Pemberton's Grammar School in Heskin, where a school party is under way celebrating the Coronation Year. The lads tucking into their cakes etc., are, from left to right; Jim Wallbank, Geoff Marsden, Tom Morris and Barrie Holding.

Another Coronation party was held in Frederick Street, with those attending ranging from a few months old into their seventies. Entertainment was provided by a street concert party. Four generations of the Green family were in attendance, including Mr Ernie Green, who still lives in the street in 2002.

I was unaware that a 'Festival' was held in the Heapey/Wheelton townships! Was this 1953 photograph a one-off only event? But so many special events took place that year. The photograph shows a wagon float for a Coronation Festival Queen.

Chorley's chosen Coronation Carnival Queen was Sheila Derbyshire, who is shown here with Queen Elect and attendants. The group are visiting Eaves Lane Hospital, and are shown with some of the staff from the hospital in August 1953.

The 1953 Coronation Queen Elect poses here with attendants soon after selection in August.

The Chorley Coronation Carnival procession began on the Flat Iron market place. Here, Queen Sheila Derbyshire's horse-drawn carriage awaits its turn to move off in the parade around the town.

The Carnival Queen's attendants, also in a horse-drawn carriage, await their turn to move off the Flat Iron in the carnival parade.

The horse-drawn carriages mingled with conventional wagon floats, which depicted activities from many of the town's organisations, such as this shown above, from the St John's Ambulance Service.

Although the name of this float or organisation cannot be identified, we do know it was part of the 1953 Carnival. Like those in the the next two floats , these angelic children will all now be 50 years older, and around the 54 to 60 age group.

Yet another float is shown on the Flat Iron, with a group of attractive young ladies on the back, ready to start off on the parade around the town. No name is visible on the float, so it is not possible to know what group this is either.

This float has 'Fairies and Elves' on it, but from which organisation? I hope that these last few photographs have not caused too much embarrassment to present-day mums, dads and grandparents who were children on the float photographs, when their own offspring find out they are there!

I'm not sure who this group on the small float represent, although their placard says 'Nursing Nuns and Red Cross Knights'. The person lying down seems to have the best job, I would suggest!

After getting into place, the floats move off the Flat Iron. Here we see the St John's Ambulance float en route around town with spectators looking on.

This float has on its side a notice saying 'The fabrics used here are by Bilanjo'. In smaller letters it says 'J. Blackledge & Sons, Park Mills, Chorley'. Brenda Westhead is on the float above the notice. Are you a spectator here? Out with the magnifying glass!

Here are a few of the many troupes of Morris Dancers who were in the 1953 carnival, passing along Market Street, near the end of High Street. This is another photograph to use the magnifying glass on!

September 1953, and the location is Heath Charnock Hospital Garden Party, with visiting Carnival Queens. In centre left is Chorley Queen Sheila Derbyshire with attendants. To the right is Adlington Queen Shirley Billington with page and attendants. Where are they all now?

In between Coronation Year and Silver Jubilee Year, we had many local Carnival and May Queens. Here we see such a group from 1958. To the left is Chorley Carnival Queen Jacqueline Turner, next to the one and only Ken Dodd, with attendants Joyce Singleton and Ann Pinsent.

To 1962 now, and another Chorley Carnival Queen, seen here with runners up for the title, after selection, is congratulated by Chorley Mayor, Councillor Alec Shepherd.

Into 1976, and Councillor Jim Moorcroft, who became Mayor of Chorley on May 17, is seen here with, from left to right; Chief Executive Officer Brian Webster, Councillor Bill Corcoran, Mayor Jim Moorcroft, Mrs Moorcroft, Mrs Keane, Councillor Ian Sellars and ex-mayor Councillor Pat Keane.

Mayor Moorcroft's year in office not only necessitated his preparatory work for the coming Silver Jubilee Year, but also his attendance at many functions. Here he is at Euxton Playschool's Summer Fair. He is holding three-year-old Katie Bankhead, in July 1976.

To celebrate the Queen's Silver Jubilee, the Duxbury Jubilee Golf Course had been completed. It was officially opened in May by Mayor Jim Moorcroft, as one of his last duties, two days before standing down.

Another children's function, this time at St Bede's Club, Clayton, where Mayor Moorcroft is officially opening a 'Tufty' group. Here, he shows, left to right, Stephanie Slater, Andrew Cooper, Richard Abraham and Joanna Whittle how the road should be crossed, in November 1976.

Two days after opening Duxbury Jubilee Golf Course, Mayor Jim Moorcroft stood down and Councillor Miss Margaret Raby became Mayor of Chorley for the Queen's Silver Jubilee Year. Here, left to right, are; Deputy Mayor Albert Lowe, Mrs Moorcroft, ex-mayor Jim Moorcroft, Mayor Councillor M. Raby and Chief Officer Mr B. Webster.

Over and above normal mayoral duties, there were also many special events to mark the Silver Jubilee Year in Chorley, including the essential present-ation of commemorative mugs to local schoolchildren. Here, Mayor Margaret Raby presents those mugs to children of Rivington Primary School.

Chorley's Silver Jubilee Carnival Queen and Princess were selected in May 1977. The popular winners were, as Queen, Miss Penny Grieveson (left), and as Princess, Miss Colette Woods (right), both from Chorley. Their photo-graphs were used in the Chorley Silver Jubilee Carnival Programme for 6 June 1977.

It's hard to imagine that this photograph was anything to do with a street party, but it was! It shows young people from Parker Street GIA in June 1977, who were coerced into doing a clean-up in the area before they had a street party – weather permitting, of course!

On carnival day, when some floats had been under preparation for weeks, it poured with rain. But it didn't deter spectators on the route. Here, on Eaves Lane, one of the 70 groups' floats passes by. This one is from Charnock Richard Parish, using a Carrington and Dewhurst's wagon.

This old Leyland 'Lioness' charabanc was occupied by ladies from All Saints' Church Mothers' Union, who were glad that their vehicle was a covered one, for the rain continued to pour.

Undaunted by the rain, the street collectors still carried out their function, in trying to collect as much money as they could for use by local charities.

This float was from Heskin Village, the vehicle, a Dodge pick-up, was supplied by Cecil Davidson (ARC) Construction Co.

This wagon depicting its 1977 date, was from Rivington Village. The theme of floats in the procession was 'any subject associated with the Queen's 25-year reign'.

This float was from Leyland Motors Bus and Truck Division.

In Market Street, and a view towards the former Electricity Showroom, plus Borough Council Offices. It's still raining heavily, as more floats pass along the street towards the Town Hall.

One of the more spectacular floats was this one from Mawdesley Youth Club. It took seven days' work to complete the float depicting Hilary's Conquest of Everest in 1953.

The Scottish and Newcastle Brewery float used umbrellas as part of their theme, which of course came in very handy in the heavy rain. Many of those on the float were as wet inside as they were outside; it was, after all, a brewery float!

Heskin Village float was one which depicted these guardsmen taking part in some royal event. But heavy rain did not enhance their busbies. Despite this, they put on a very impressive display.

Another very impressive float was that from Euxton Parish. It depicted the theme of the Prince of Wales' Investiture, and took some weeks to build, complete with a replica Caernarvon Castle.

Chorley Silver Jubilee Carnival procession came to end in Astley Park, where it still continued to rain on that 6 June day. In the arena, the elected Chorley Carnival Queen Penny Grieveson and the Princess Colette Woods, were crowned by The Brothers signing group

Another rather special gift was this crochet image of the Queen, which was presented to the mayor. This image is still in good condition in 2002.

Mayor Margaret Raby received many items relating to the Queen's Silver Jubilee, which were distributed appropriately. This large decorated cake was presented to the mayor by Mrs Bagot of Hall's Bakery, Chorley. The small crown, cushion and badges on the cake survived into Golden Jubilee Year.

The many functions attended by the mayor during Silver Jubilee Year 1977 were, to say the least, varied. From school visits as shown here, to having lunch with, the Queen in Preston's County Hall on 20 June (which I cannot find photographs of).

Another rained-off party took place in Charnock Richard, when the street party, due to be held in Town Lane, had to be relocated to the *Hinds Head pub.*

As a bonus for Chorley, and its Jubilee Carnival Queen herself, later in 1977 Miss Penny Grieveson was voted Carnival Queen of Great Britain, as shown here – which was a nice way to wind down the celebrations which had taken place over the year.

At the Royal Ordnance Factory club on Euxton Lane, a Jubilee Queen was chosen during 1977 instead of the normal Miss ROF Chorley. The winning Queen and runners up are shown here.

SOME BUILDINGS RECALLED

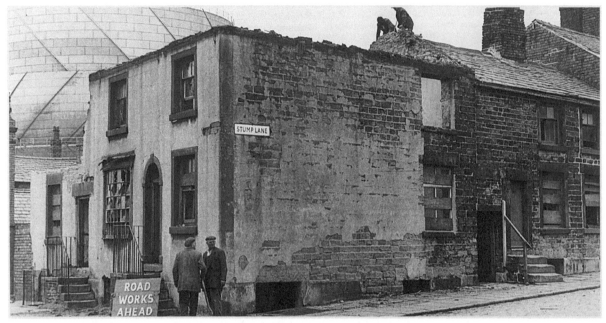

The early 1950s saw much old property being cleared away in Chorley. One such location was in Bengal Street, at its corner with Stump Lane. These interesting old houses, including the one to the left, have cellars, and were built of stone.

Not far from the previous location, in Hollinshead Street close to the chapel, stood these buildings, demolished about 1950. They were once a large double-fronted house, called Hollinshead House (hence the street name). The building to the right of the arch remains in 2002.

Still in Hollinshead Street. Remember how one cottage was left standing for a time, when the whole row, from opposite Fellery Street to Bengal Street had been demolished? It stood on the corner, where the garage stands. Note the Parish Institute and Park Street School in the distance.

Out of the town centre for this view. Any ideas where? Well, the huts were formerly used as part of an army detention centre during the war. It was of course at Lower Healey (Bleachworks). The huts were used by squatters into the 1950s, when the people living there were rehoused.

I know that not very much of this building is visible, but if I say that the Co-op milk float is loading up at this place, I suspect you will have some idea where it was. I am told that it was at their main depot in Little Steeley Lane, taken in March 1958. Chorley Co-op was established in 1887.

Now here's one building I bet you won't recall! You can see where it was from the street names on the corner, at the end of Moor Road. Whatever its origins, it was certainly a grand building of later 19th century date. It was used by Birkacre Bleach Works for some years.

Mr Brown gave his name to the street, and lived here at Eastview House. He was a cotton manufacturer, starting his business in Parker Street, then setting up the mill behind the house, later to become Chortex. The house later became a Boys' Club. Photograph taken in 1955.

Chorley in the early 19th century had many domestic manufacturers of cotton, such as spinners and weavers, who worked in house cellars. Most were centred in the Bolton Street area, but those in the photograph stood at the corner of Harpers Lane with Botany Brow until the early 1960s.

Clearance of old property in the Bolton Street, Albion Street and Bolton Road areas in the late 1950s and early 1960s allowed this view to be taken of the Lodging House that was in King Street.

Not quite so much of a 'building' perhaps, but I feel worthy of its inclusion, due to it being so much a part of Chorley social history in the 1950s. Yes, it's Chorley's second open-air swimming pool at Hartwood Hall Hotel, which was open to the public for a time.

Another of Chorley's halls which was demolished due to being in poor condition, was Higher Burgh Hall, here photographed when occupied in the 1960s. It was a site with important associations for the Roman Catholic faith in Chorley.

This is a photograph of a major nostalgic order! It shows the demolition of the Royal in Market Street in July 1960. We are looking from the screen end, outwards to Market Street. The lower cross girders supported the balcony – the upper one, the 'monkey rack'.

Surely the old Police Station looks infinitely better than the present-day building! Here is a good example of the loss of character in the town's buildings. The building was, of course, on St Thomas's Road. It was demolished in the mid-1960s. Adjoining the Police Station to the right, were these buildings (below) which fronted on to the Town Hall Square.

The site of the Police Station and Town Hall Square buildings, plus those to the south side of Farrington Street (including my parents' house, visible to the left), were all cleared by the end of 1961, ready to start foundation work for the new Police Station.

In Market Street, another building of character was the Williams Deacons Bank. This was between Woolworth's and the archway to St Mary's Church. It was demolished in the later 1960s (at the other side of Woolworth's, the stone-built District Bank was also demolished later).

Chorley's bus station is shown here in 1964 – a time when it was overdue for renewal. Demolition began later in the year, into 1965, when the new (present-day) station was built, soon to be relocated. This was a view of the platforms from Cleveland Street.

Another view of the pre-1965 bus station, this time from Union Street. Out-of-service buses parked between the platforms and Union Street. The platforms were arranged so that buses ran through them, as opposed to the present day station, where the buses run in front first.

Out of town a little now, and to Bagganley Lane, where Bagganley Hall stood from the 17th century. The M61 hard shoulder and verge had to run over the site (as if it couldn't have been slightly realigned!), so we lost yet another hall in 1967. This view shows the back of the building.

I spoke of this building a little while ago, when the milk float was the subject. This view, from the Lyons Lane end of Little Steeley Lane shows the headquarters building, with dance hall on the top floor, of the Chorley Co-op. This too was demolished in the 1960s.

This 1960s view looks down Water Street (often referred to as Chorley Bottoms), in the River Chor valley. The picture shows the former gasworks of 19th century origins. Climbing the crane and gantry was one of our 'dares' as boys. The large building was the Retort House.

This view of 1970 has some interesting elements. It is Church Brow, filled in, to become Church Steps. The road passed to the left, where the car is parked. To the right, Hollinshead Street and the two houses which have become the Swan pub. The original Swan is to the right.

The subject of this photograph is perhaps not too easy to recognise immediately, but the decorative plasterwork each side may help. It is, of course, the interior of the former Odeon, looking towards the screen. Work to convert it into a bingo hall is under way in this picture of 1973.

Although I have referred to the Parish Church Girls' School previously in another context, here it is again, this time viewed from the front, in Water Street. The photograph dates from about 1974.

Remember Gillibrand Hall carriage drive that was gifted to the council with woodland? It was all built over! This was the viaduct that carried the north entrance drive to the hall near to the Gillibrand Arms pub. It was demolished in about 1976.

I know I speak so much of character in the town and how it's being lost, with so many interesting buildings been demolished etc, but here is another example, as demolished in the later 1970s. It is the former Barclays Bank building now rebuilt in a modern style.

I suppose most of us growing up through the '50s and '60s, learned to swim here, at Chorley Baths, at a time when there was no additional pool to the south end for small children. This view dates from 1975, when the children's pool had been added, but there were no squash courts yet!

Inside the baths it was never really warm, and the seats around the main pool, shown here, were cold to sit on. But so many of us got our first length certificate, swimming from this near, shallow end, to the deep end in the distance – the site of the diving boards.

This was a location where again many of us spent happy times, either splashing about or, if we could, sailing boats. It was the Astley Park paddling pool, now destroyed. Yet it was gifted to Chorley people by a local organisation. A replacement would surely be very acceptable!

One building that certainly should have been retained (which was also gifted to Chorley people), was the Public Library in Avondale Road. It would have filled an admirable role as the town's Heritage Centre, a facility which is sadly lacking in Chorley. Photograph taken in the mid-1970s.

During the 1970s we saw several mill buildings demolished in and around the town. My interest in industrial history meant that it fell to me to record the passing of these buildings, such as this one in Cowling Brow, formerly Redan Mill, and part of the Cobden's mill complex.

I saved this 'best till last' example of heritage lost in Chorley, and, no, I will not mention 'character' this time! It says it for itself. This was Eaves Lane Hospital, part of our Victorian heritage, just bulldozed away, when surely this frontage building could have been converted to other use, perhaps as flats. It's a point to ponder! Photograph was taken in the 1970s.

The 1970s were a busy years for the author, reviewing so-called protected buildings in Chorley and compiling a report. One of the publicity photographs, shown here, shows the author in front of such a building, which later was restored, to become the Swan with Two Necks pub in Hollinshead Street.

VIPS AND OTHER VISITORS

You can't get any higher a VIP than the Queen herself, can you? The photograph shows her having just boarded the Royal Train at Leyland. She had been to Chorley – Anderton, in fact – to open the M61 services building there. Many Chorley people were at the service station to see the Queen on this visit in October 1971.

I have often wondered how many people were waiting outside the new St Michael's School in October 1965, as we all waited for Princess Margaret to arrive and officially open the school. After unveiling a plaque in the foyer, she made a tour of the school.

Four years later, in March 1969, Princess Margaret was in the Chorley area again. This time she came to Brinscall to open another new school. This was St John's CE/Methodist School. The school was reported to be the first combined school in England.

Inside the school, the customary plaque was unveiled to mark the official opening, but the school had been open unofficially since 1968, the year before the Princess came. In this view, the Princess chats with pupils in one of the classrooms.

Back in time a little now, with the following photographs. Here, ten years before he became Prime Minister, is Mr Harold Wilson in Chorley, shaking hands with Mayor Mrs Edith May Edwards in March 1954.

Here we see Prime Minister Clement Attlee in the centre, with Wilf Rawcliffe to the left, and Clifford Kenyon MP to the right. Mr Attlee was Churchill's deputy in wartime, and his opponent after. He stood down as Prime Minister in December 1955, seven months after this photograph was taken.

In this 1959 photograph, we see a stage we were all familiar with. It is the former Tudor Ballroom in Gillibrand Street. Centre stage is Mr Hugh Gaitskill, Leader of the Labour Party in the 1950s, who was beaten in the 1959 General Election, by Harold Macmillan.

Back to the 1950s again, and a showbusiness visitor who was in Chorley on several occasions. This was Harry Korris (on the left). He was probably best known for his part in the radio shows of the '40s and '50s, called *ITMA* which starred Tommy Handley. Photograph taken in May 1956.

At the 1958 Chorley carnival, the guest of honour was Ken Dodd. He is seen here on the arena stage of the carnival field. He's not changed a lot since that time, has he?

This photograph was taken at Messrs Coopers Ltd, Chortex factory, usually called the 'towel factory'. The factory had many celebrity visitors. They were usually in shows in Blackpool at the time. In October 1957, a young Bob Monkhouse poses with two of the weavers.

This photograph is also at the Chortex towel factory. The visiting celebrity is another 'younger version'! This time it's Dora Bryan (in the centre), who came in February 1958. Her most recent television appearances have been in the ever-popular show *Last of the Summer Wine*.

The same location as the previous two photographs, the Chortex factory. The most recognisable person in this photograph is the late Tommy Cooper, on the left. Right of centre at the back is Michael Medwin, comedy actor in many films. The VIP pair are shown here with factory employees.

In the '50s and '60s, a popular radio show was *Down Your Way*, with interviewer Franklyn Engelman. The show was recorded in Chorley for the *Light Programme* in March 1960. The photograph shows Mr Engelman (centre), with Chorley Librarian Mr Blackburn outside Astley Hall.

In *c.*1953/54 Hylda Baker made one of her regular visits to Chorley, as seen in this photograph. She was a great supporter and fundraiser for children afflicted with autism. It is believed that she was in Chorley at some sort of fund-raising event. No other information is known.

There were many current affairs programmes on television during the early 1960s. One of these had a reporter called Julian Pettifer. He is seen here (to the right), in Dole Lane, Chorley in 1963. The subject under discussion was the introduction of personal radios for the police.

In August 1956, at Chorley Town Hall, top male singer of the time Frankie Vaughan came along to perform, to help raise money for a local Boys' Club. He is seen here at that venue. Frank was a big fundraiser to the cause of young people, and helped set up social and sporting clubs.

Chorley carnival of August 1962 had as its Queen Pat Leadbetter, shown here on the left, next to the mayor and mayoress, and Miss Great Britain. To the right is visitor Nicholas Parsons, who played straight man in several TV comedy programmes – notably opposite Arthur Haines – prior to his more recent career as a game show host.

The film showing at the Odeon cinema in May 1955 was *The Colditz Story*, starring Lionel Jeffries, who visited when the film was on. He is seen here shaking hands with the mayor. Lionel Jeffries' father was Superintendent at Highways Hostel in Balshaw Lane, Euxton.

In the later 1950s, a personality dominating our wireless sets was singer and comedienne Tessie O'Shea. She visited Chorley to attend the mayor's charity ball, in the Town Hall. The Mayor was Mr W. Lowe, seen here with Mrs Lowe and Tessie, during the charity auction.

Gracie Fields came to Chorley several times, including in 1937 when she sang at the ROF Gala. Here, at Greenfield Mill in late 1949, Gracie signs her autograph whilst talking to weaver Mrs Ogden, mother of Eric, Hilda, Jimmy and Brian. (The autograph book still survives in 2002).

CHORLEY PUBS REMEMBERED

I start with a pub which teeters on the brink of extinction – one which has been closed and boarded-up for some time now. As to whether or not the Talbot Arms in Botany Brow will ever reopen, is anyone's guess, but, like the pub in Union Street, the former Imperial, I doubt it!

A similar two-storey building to the Talbot was this Park Road pub – the Townley Arms – situated between Commercial Road and Astley Street. Like the Talbot, it was a deceptively large pub.

Astley Street formed a crossroads with Parker Street. The Bay Horse was on the corner (the white building). It had two entrances, but that in Parker Street was the main one and postal address. Former landlady Sybil Flanagan tells me that it closed down in 1969. It has since been demolished. Further down the street was the Prince Consort until 1961.

One of three former stage coach inns was the Red Lion. Its original entrance was in Market Street, later Mealhouse Lane. It was demolished in the early 1960s. A large yard behind the pub was used for horse stabling, with a small pub across the yard from the front house.

That pub across the yard was called the Red Lion Tap, in Back Mount – popular with locals, who included my father. We lived about a hundred yards away. The US forces also liked the pub in the 1940s. It was the first pub I went into as a boy, sent for a jug of beer to make shandies at home.

When the Tap was being demolished in the early 1960s, this photograph was obtained, showing the emerging Town Hall above the pub's front wall. To the left, the front house is still standing. All the site was later taken up by the White Hart, which in 2002 has regained its original name.

In St Thomas's Road was a small pub similar in size to the Tap. It stood opposite the old Police Station, and next to Sumner's Corn Mill entrance gates. It was the Court Tavern – popular with young men of the 1950s and '60s, and with the police, for their cigarettes and crisps!

Clifford Street, despite its length, was not, surprisingly, blessed with many pubs. The main one, shown with the Bed-and-Breakfast sign in the early 1980s was the Robin Hood. It was famous around Lancashire for its crown green bowling competitions.

This is that famous bowling green behind the Robin Hood. We can see the backs of houses on Clifford Street. The photograph was taken from the railway embankment. On occasion, I saw spectators 10 deep around the green, watching competitions. My aunt lived nearby, so I had family access.

Although on the corner of Clifford Street, the front door to the Cordwainer's Arms was actually in Livesey Street. After its closure, it was a cafeteria for a time, but was demolished when Hill Street and Livesey Street were cleared for the shopping mall. Photograph from the early 1960s.

In New Market Street was one of the most popular pubs in the town centre, which organised many charity events and fund-raising activities. It was the Fazackerley Arms, seen here at the end of the '60s, the front having been repainted, and awaiting new signage etc.

This is the front of the 'Fazack' that most people will recognise, when its name was over the door and its notices in the windows. The pub had entertainment that catered for all tastes. Its demise was quite a blow to a great many regulars.

At the other side of the Market Place, until the mid-1950s was this pub – the Clarence, seen here after its closure. The pub was demolished and new shop premises built on the site.

Back in Market Street again, near the bottom of Chapel Street, in-between Moore's shop and that of Mangnall's, recently relocated, was this small pub. It was called the Waterloo. The landlord for many years was former boxer Mr Gent.

Another Market Street corner was occupied by this pub, which was actually in Gillibrand Street. It was called the Wellington. It closed in the 1960s and became a shop. That premises was demolished in 1999, and redevelopment of the site started in March 2002.

A little further up Market Street and on yet another corner was this large pub, on the corner of Cunliffe Street. It was, of course, the Cunliffe Arms. This, too, became a shop after it had closed. It was known for many years as Poppycock.

Turning right out of Railway Street we arrive at Lyons Lane corner, where this pub stood, which closed in the late 1950s. It was called the Castle Inn.

Turning left out of Railway Street, into Lyons Lane, and over the railway bridge, to the right one came to this former pub. It was called the White Lion. Although empty for some time after closure, it is now used as a mosque.

To the south side of the Castle Inn was what, at first glimpse, seems to be just an alley. But it was in fact a street, called Whittle Street, which led to the Railway Wagon Works, run by a Mr Whittle. In this view, the street name is visible on the pub gable end.

Returning back down Lyons Lane one came to Brooke Street on the left. On this corner was a pub called the Victoria. For some reason it had the nickname of 'Red House'.

Further up Brooke Street, on the corner of Towneley Street, was this pub called the Queens. On two sides of the pub were rows of terraced houses, and it was very much a 'local' pub, which was used by people living close by. The pub and the houses have now been demolished.

A pub near the top of Standish Street was called the Hare and Hounds. It had an interesting nickname, for it was a pub which saw many fights. Because of these battles, it was referred to as the 'War Office'. Shown here with scaffolding in front.

Where Lyons Lane joined Bolton Street was a pub called the Plough. This name was later changed to the Borough, a name it carried till closure. This view dates from the 1960s.

Directly across the road from the Borough, was the Princess Royal. It was one of those pubs near the 'car watching' location, like the Borough across the road – an area we knew as 'up Duke'. It was also very close to the Plaza cinema.

Across from the Plaza and the Princess Royal, was a pub on the corner of King Street called the White Bear Inn. This survived into the 1960s, despite the adjoining property being demolished – as the pub eventually was.

These last few photographs are of pubs just out of town, but in Chorley Borough. This first one was on the old Chorley to Blackburn road at Wheelton. It is the former Red Cat. Since its closure as a pub, it has become an Italian restaurant.

To Euxton now, and the A49 Wigan Road. Here is another pub which has become an Italian restaurant, known as Papa Luigi's. It was the former Anderton Arms, as shown in the photograph. The Andertons were the Lords of the Manor of Euxton (pronounced Exton).

The Talbot Arms in Balshaw Lane achieved popularity in the war years, when there was a hostel and a US army camp close by. As the pub was the camp's 'local', it was always full of GIs with their cigars and cigarettes. It became known as 'Smokey Joes'. The photograph shows the old pub with the new one to replace it, almost complete, just visible to the right.

M61 Construction, and
Local Changes

We first look at the building of the M61 from the south side of Chorley, in the borough parish of Anderton, where Lancashire now meets Greater Manchester. Here a service station was built. The columns in the photograph are part of it. In the distance, Rivington Pike, as viewed in 1968.

At 'Major Bottoms' in Anderton, the lane was diverted. It used to swing to the left towards the distant pub, at the top of Babylon Lane, but was diverted to the right, and a new bridge built over the 'motor road'. This photograph was taken in 1968.

In quiet Limbrick – a deep valley through which the River Yarrow flows – a high bridge was built, to carry the motorway across the valley. The bridge is shown here nearing completion in 1968. The old cottages in the foreground have been demolished, and a new building constructed.

Moving to Crosse Hall now, a place many of us recall with 'Johnny's Brow' and the 'rushpit', plus of course Crosse Hall itself, or at least the remains of it. The M61 now passes across the middle of the scene, with a long bridge over it, forming the modern 'brow'.

North of Crosse Hall is Lower Healey. This view looks over the canal bridge in Froom Street and across the 'east valley' towards the 'Nab'. I was working at Lower Healey Works at this time, to the left. Drainage work for the road is under way in 1967.

From near the same location as the previous photograph, this telephoto view shows a very controversial quarry on the 'Nab', from which stone was removed for motorway hardcore. There were many fears that the site would not be restored, but, fortunately, it was. Photograph was taken in 1968.

Talbot Mill main offices were in Bagganley Lane, in which stood the 17th-century Bagganley Hall. This listed building with its barns and farm was demolished for the motorway, when surely a slight diversion could have been made to retain it.

Bagganley Lane ended with a trackway that ran through Temple Fields. As the new road was to cut through this trackway as well, a subway had to be built under the new road. Here, part of that subway is in place, near the old bridge over Black Brook.

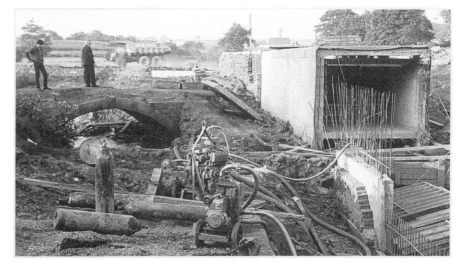

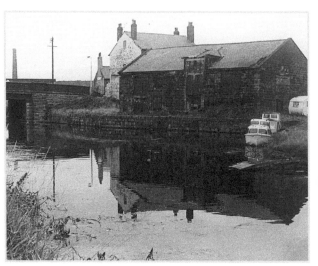

Botany Bay, Chorley 1966. This wharf with 19th-century warehouse was described as 'Chorley's port'. It was a busy place from the 1790s. It was said to be harder working here than in the Australian Penal Colony, hence the nickname! The warehouse was demolished in 1968.

As the new subway was built and subsequently covered over to form the new carriageway, this view was obtained from the new road verge, looking across Temple Fields to the works of T. Witter and Co at Heapey.

Viewed from Bagganley Lane canal bridge, and looking to the north before the trees became too overgrown. The new motorway bridge over the canal is in use, but not complete. In the distance, the former Heapey Road Chapel is visible.

As work on the motorway arrived at Botany, it was made known that many houses would have to be demolished to make way for the new motorway. This photograph was taken from the canal bridge looking towards the houses which had to go, on both sides of Botany Brow.

When the houses as seen previously had been cleared, the area between the road and the railway line was levelled, preparing for the removal of the railway embankment and the 99-year-old nine arch viaduct, which was to be demolished by explosives.

Whilst preparations for the removal of the railway embankment and viaduct were under way, at the other side of the road bridge the old warehouse was demolished to make way for a new road bridge, to cross both canal and motorway. Also visible is Talbot Mill in the distance.

With the old warehouse gone, work on the new Botany Bridge got under way in earnest. Here, new concrete bridge supports have been cast, but the old road is still in use to the left. Note that early Chorley discotheque in Knowley Brow – the Odd Spot.

This view from the Knowley side of the canal looks back towards Chorley. The old road bridge is still in use, and the steelwork for the new canal and motorway bridge over Botany Bay is well under way.

This was the sad moment which, reluctantly, many of us waited for so long to see one Sunday morning in November 1968. It was the moment of demolition by explosives of the nine-arch Botany Viaduct, built in 1899. The photograph was taken from the roadside at the bottom of Botany Brow.

When the smoke and dust had died away after the explosions, the two ends of the viaduct were still standing, as were two of the centre columns. The decking over the canal had done its job, and very little masonry had fallen into it.

Both ends of the viaduct survived the demolition explosion. The biggest surviving portion was that at the Chorley end. Shown here shortly after demolition, about one-third of the last arch has survived.

On completion of the new Botany Bridge, the old road was closed and the railway embankment removed, allowing the full width of the new carriageways to be made. In this 1969 view, the new bridge is still not quite finished. The old Botany Bridge is to the right of centre.

With the new bridge open, one could photograph what was going on to the north. We can see that the embankment has gone, and two carriageways have been created, running north to Hartwood bridges and roundabout. The old road is still in place at the bottom of the photograph.

Moving to the north of Chorley, here at Whittle Springs, where the Leeds-Liverpool Canal (to the right), meets the old Lancaster Canal. In the distance over Town Lane, a new road bridge is being built for the M61.

From that new bridge over Town Lane, this was the view looking down on to Town Lane, with the Lancaster Canal bridge still in place to the right of centre. This did not survive for very long, for the road was widened at this bend.

The Whittle Hills proved to be a difficult obstacle for the motorway builders. It was here that a whole hillside of rock had to be removed to allow the new road to pass. Here, the depth of the excavation can be seen, before a new bridge was built.

A few months after the previous photograph was taken, this view shows the progress made, with a new bridge built across the gap cut through the hill. The stonework to the lower left, above the pipes, was the remains of the former St Helen's Well.

The old Lancaster Canal was cut through several times by the new motorway, and many of the canal bridges were demolished. The road caused great damage to areas of historic importance. Here, the old bridge at Radburn, Brindle, has a temporary reprieve, as the canal basin is filled in.

This is another view of Radburn Bridge, with only the parapets still visible. A new bridge is being built to the left, which, when complete, will see the old bridge demolished.

Past Radburn Bridge en route to Walton Summit terminus and basin, the old Lancaster Canal passed through pleasant countryside, as shown here, by Brindle Waterworks bridge. This section was drained, but the bridge remains today.

The three-armed terminus of the south end of the Lancaster Canal at Walton Summit was in use from the early 1800s. From here, a horse-drawn railway ran to Preston, five miles further north. The coming of the M61 motorway saw this terminus drained and bulldozed level.

Returning to Chorley, and a view taken from close to Crosse Hall bridge, the former 'Johnny's Brow', looking towards Froom Street and the Talbot Mill. The motorway's northern end (Anderton to Bamber Bridge), covering 13 miles, is completed and due to open.

The opening of the northern section of the Manchester to Preston motorway took place on 20 November 1969, by the Rt Honourable Mr F. Mulley MP, Minister of Transport. Here, the official ribbon is cut. The remaining south end section was completed later, and opened in December 1970.

PEOPLE AND EVENTS

No – these are not recruits for a 'Dad's Army' squad, but are cadets who are on camp and taking part in a shooting competition. Many of them, if not all, are from Chorley, and will be recognised by many readers. The photograph dates from the late 1940s.

A double queue at the Pavilion cinema in April 1954. On the left are people nearest to the paybox. Note the typical 1950s gaberdine macs. Lawrence Lee (of Woolley's toyshop) and Jimmy Clarkson are in the centre of the photograph. It must have been a good film!

Thought to have been taken in 1954, this is a group of employees and families from Miller's shop in New Market Street, ready for a day's outing. Two former school friends from Hollinshead Street School are; second from left, John Campbell, and Eric Greenway sixth from left.

We often went to swimming galas at Chorley baths in the 1950s. Here at one such event, is an escapology performance from Lawrence Lee, in the trunk, and Phillip Croasdale of Springfield Road. With the mayor of Chorley looking on.

In 1954, Sir Robert Fossett's circus came to Chorley, and set up a marquee on the Flat Iron. The elephants came by special rail wagons, and were off-loaded near Chorley station – here being watched by a group of children. The elephants walked through Market Street to the Flat Iron.

An amateur boxing competition was held at the Town Hall in October 1955. Here, some of the boy competitors pose for the camera.

Coach trips were popular in the 1950s. Here one such trip is about to set off from the Grammar School steps in Union Street in September 1956.

This 1956 photograph shows a group of 1st Loyal Cadets in Chorley, who were taking part in a pilot scheme for the Duke of Edinburgh Awards. The officer with cross belt on the front row is Mr L. Chapman.

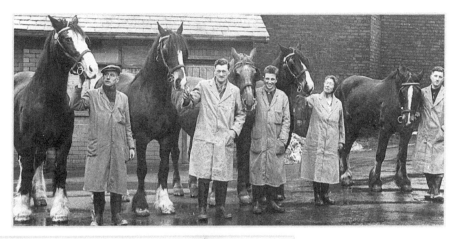

March 1958, and a scene which heralded the end of an era. The photograph shows horses of Chorley Co-operative Society, which had been employed on milk deliveries in and around Chorley for many years, on the first day of their official retirement.

The photograph was taken at Chorley Football Club's ground, Victory Park, possibly in May of 1958. It shows a group of supporters for the Chorley team, the Magpies, awaiting the start of an important match.

This coach party is one organised by Brooke Street Working Men's Club in 1958. It is about to set off for Blackpool, on what appears to be a rather wet day, from alongside the Brookes Arms pub.

Yet another coach party are about to set off on a seaside trip, most likely to Blackpool again, for it is only an hour or so away from Chorley. Notice the 'evacuee-type' labels being worn, so children would not get lost.

Believed to be a performance of *Miss Hook of Holland* by members of the Chorley Operatic Society, the photograph shows members of the cast on stage during early April 1962.

The first buses without conductors were introduced in the Chorley area in October 1958. They were single deck only at first. The photograph, taken a few days after their introduction, shows a Mrs Ince and daughter Christine, 'paying on entry', at the end of October 1958.

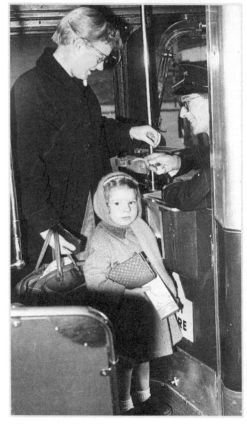

The early 1960s was a time when mills were on short-time due to excessive importation of cheaper cotton goods. Local mills protested against these imports by organising marches and lobbying etc. This June 1962 photograph shows a local group about to leave on a protest march.

The same type of protest, in late June of 1962, this time at some unknown local mill. The protest banner over the car has a clever innuendo relating to a film with Bob Hope in it, but it also implies that there is 'No Hope' for Lancashire mills, due to Hong Kong imports.

Chorley's old bus station survived until 1965, when it was replaced with a new one, which in 2002 is to be replaced and relocated. The photograph shows the official opening ceremony in 1965, with Chorley Mayor Ian Sellars in attendance.

There were many local lads who, in the 1960s, formed their own small groups, and played at venues around the area. One such group is shown here. They were called Blues by Five. Photographed in November 1965.

The old Police Station closed in 1965, prior to demolition. The police relocated to Woodlands Hostel site, where they shared the site with the Post Office, which was also undergoing alterations at the time. Here, new Panda cars with drivers line up at the Woodlands site.

Walking Day in Chorley during 1967. Here, part of the procession passes the end of St Thomas's Road. The children are from St George's Church.

Another group of children from St George's Church approach the Town Hall, also in 1967. At each end of the leading rope and line of children, are, to the left, Rona Halton, and to the right Joan Berry.

This group of young people are taking part in a 24-hour vigil, calling attention to the 'War on Want'. The date is April 1968, and the location is the end of Church Street with Chapel Street.

Another Walking Day photo-graph now, and this time I am uncertain which church the children are from, although I am informed that it was probably taken at the 1968 procession.

This Walking Day photograph of 1970 shows children from St James's Church as they pass the Town Hall. School friend John Campbell is below Mayor Rowlandson.

This group of walkers, also in 1970, are from the Church of All Saints', and are passing the main gates of Astley Park. To the right, Mrs Joan Prescott, with floppy hat, former work colleague at ROF Chorley.

The greatest change we had in 1971, was the introduction of decimal currency. We had been told in 1970 what the new coins would be like and their values, but it was still hard to accept. Our picture shows a tea-towel reminder of those values, as seen on the Flat Iron market.

Although I am unaware at which venue this stage production of *The Desert Song* was being performed, the date is April 1968. It has been suggested that the cast may have been St Mary's Operatic Society, but this is not certain.

On first seeing this photograph, I thought it might be a Pied Piper in Chorley! Taken in August 1969, the location seems to be on Thorn Hill, off Eaves Lane. It is likely that whatever was going on, it was associated with St Joseph's Church, which is close by.

One of the candidates in the Parliamentary Election of 1970, was Conservative Mrs Connie Monks, wife of well-known newsagent Jack Monks, who had his shop in St Thomas's Road. Mrs Monks was successfully elected MP for Chorley, and is seen here with supporters after the announcement of the result.

Taken at the Odeon cinema paybox, which had been altered to a shop as well, by mid-February 1971. The admission prices are five shillings in the stalls, two shillings for children and one shilling for pensioners.

In the early 1970s I became founder chairman the Astley Hall Society and vice-chair of the Chorley Civic Trust. Here in 1975 I host the official opening of Astley Hall courtyard to the public. My daughter, Carole Smith, presents flowers to Mayoress Mrs Keane, with Mayor Pat Keane to the right, and the author further to the right.

In 1975 the go-ahead was given by the CLDC to do a dig at Astley Hall Farm. This was led by J. Hallam, Archaeological Consultant to the CLDC. In this photograph, right to left; Mr Hallam, the author (representing Chorley Historical and Archaeological Society) and Jen Lewis, of West Lancs. Archaeological Society.

As Chair of the Astley Hall Society, it was good to have been involved with the organisation for the concert given by the wonderful band, Patriots of Music, from East Detroit, USA, in Astley Park on 4 July 1976. The location is near Astley Hall.

Another Astley Hall Society event held in 1976, was an Elizabethan Evening, where the St Nicholas Singers performed. They are shown here in the courtyard at Astley Hall. To the right of this line-up is another of my daughters, Dianne Smith.

In May 1977, a reception for Chorley FC was held in the Town Hall. Here, members of the club pose with the mayor, Councillor Jim Moorcroft, and the mayoress. To the right front is Councillor Corcoran, with Mrs Corcoran to the left.

Early in Silver Jubilee year, the local Ranger group Queen's Guides, visited the Town Hall, where they were shown the civic regalia. Hosting the event was Mayor Jim Moorcroft, with Mayoress Mrs Margaret Moorcroft in attendance.

Following a street party in Parker Street in 1977, and May Festival in 1978, a bonfire spectacular with a torchlight procession, stalls and fireworks, took place in November 1978. Included in the procession was this dragon, who was given the name of

The Parker Street GIA had connections with the Arts Association, who set up a scheme called an 'Arts Development Area' (ADA), and the Parker Street action group area was selected for this pilot scheme. One of the 1978 events was a pottery workshop, shown in the photograph.

For the Parker Street residents, a new character made its appearance for the May Festival of 1979. This was another dragon, called 'Parker MkII', seen here, with body uncovered, as legs only should be showing. Here seen approaching the Parker Street green.

As well as ADA involvement, Parker Street residents held fund-raising activities such as a 'Raise the Roof' event, held on Astley Park, to raise funds for Park Street Church. This was shown on Granada TV. Our photograph shows a circus workshop under way in early 1980.

The links the Parker Street community committee established took arts outside the GIA area, into the town. Here, in Fazackerley Street in early 1980, a Mummers Play, *St George and the Dragon*, was performed. In 1981, the committee assisted with the first 'playbus' in the area.

ROF Chorley

This chapter uses photographs taken at ROF Chorley, showing how they were taken at a great variety of events and activities, in addition to those taken of ammunition production. Here, factory director Mr Purcell makes a presentation to a Fire Brigade officer in the early 1970s.

One of the aspects of working in Government Service for many years was the presentation of the long-service award, the Imperial Service Medal. Here, staff from the Instrument Shop, including; Johnny Good, Frank Keeling and Ray Branston, pose after getting their medals.

Many of the medal presentations in the 1980s, took place without families in attendance. Here staff from the Drawing Office pose with their medals. Including Brian Booth and Joe Deakin.

Another Imperial Service Medal presentation – this time for Safety Department staff. From the right, Peter Iddon, George Brooks, Director Terry Jebb and Ted Kavanagh. Of the four, it is probably Ted who will be best recalled by a large number of people. We all knew when he was around!

Many Imperial Service Medal presentations were held with families present, as shown in this photograph. They usually took place in what was called the South Side Canteen, now used as BAe offices on Euxton lane. Like most of the photographs here, this one was taken in the 1970s.

Most usually recalled, perhaps, for his time on process group five, this is Fred Bullock. He is shown here with family after receiving his Imperial Service Medal.

A final medal presentation now, with Director Mr Purcell presenting the actual medal. The medal stated the recipient's name around the edge, and on the reverse stated; 'For Faithful Service'. It was not just a long-service medal, however, but reflected much more. This ceremony ended in the later 1980s.

Taken in the factory Training School, Building 8A3, in December 1974, this photograph shows a group of employees receiving a certificate for a training course, from director Mr Lavin. Included here are Bill Worden, Ted Steele, Rod Exley, Fred Taylor and Brian Metters.

Just to show that during the 1970s – specifically 1976, when this photograph was taken – the ROF at Chorley was producing conventional ammunition. Here, warheads for the 'Rapier' missile are being inspected on factory production Group 8.

This group had been taking part in an Indoor Sports Awards presentation at the factory Sports and Social Club on Euxton Lane, in May of 1977. Included are Jack Piggot and Ken Hall. Sitting on the floor in the centre is factory Director Jim Lavin.

First Aid training was always encouraged on the ROF production groups. Groups had teams that competed against each other, as well as with other ROFs. Some of the First Aiders are seen here, outside Group Three West canteen in the mid-1970s.

In this group photograph showing First Aiders again, a team from ROF Chorley, after winning a trophy for their abilities. Included in the photograph are; Peter Smallwood, Vic Elmore, with factory Director Jim Lavin in the centre.

Apprentice training was another subject high on the agenda at ROF Chorley. Each year, until the 1980s, annual awards took place in the South Side Canteen, shown here in the early 1970s. At each presentation, a visiting VIP, usually from the services, presented the awards.

At the Annual Apprentice Awards, parents attended the function, which had a buffet laid on. Here, a group of apprentices from 1977 pose in South Side Canteen, wearing the fashionable wide ties typical of the decade.

As well as visiting services personnel coming to apprentice awards, sometimes other personalities attended. Here in the apprentice training school in 1977, is former Preston North End and England footballer Tom Finney, himself a plumber by trade.

As stated earlier, photographs seem to have been taken for so many different events at the ROF, some of which are unidentifiable! Here, in front of two factory buses, staff from the Transport Department pose for the camera, for some unknown event in 1977.

At the ROF factory in 2002 there is now only one production area remaining – the former Group One, but in the 1970s inter-group and factory sporting competitions were commonplace. Here a team in 1978 includes Martin Cowburn, Dave Whalley and John Smith – all former work colleagues.

In 1979, the Calibration Department staff at ROF Chorley pose for a retirement photograph outside building 3J21. Many local men are in the photograph, including the author, to the right of the third row.

Here is another photograph taken at the training school, just into 1980, with Training Officer Mills on the front row. Amongst those attending the course are Ellen Gillett, Jim Hickman, Geoff Kitchen, Stan McCloud and Ian Bagshaw.

Another annual competition was for Good Housekeeping. Again this was held between production groups. The winners' cup was held by the production group for a year. Here Kath Eccleston, of Group 3 east, receives the cup from A/D Mr Donovan, on her right, with Mr E. Lloyd to her left.

Winning the Good Housekeeping cup was always good for the morale of a group. Here, we see Edna Clewarth receiving the cup from A/D Trevor Collier, in the early 1980s. Left to right are: K. Bradburn, Edna Clewarth, T. Collier, S. Mosley and B. Mahoney.

This group are standing in front of the Administration building, 10C18, and are mainly from the Safety Department. The occasion is the retirement presentation of Keith Bowe in the early 1980s. Also in the photograph, Fred Blackledge, Tony Dakin, Wilma Gregory, Eddy Davenport and Danny Donegan.

As well as men's football teams at the ROF, there were women's teams. One such team is shown here in the early-eighties. Some of the girls are; Janet Shirley, Jean Armitage, Winnie Christie. To the left is Harry Hall, and to the right Chris Denton.

I had to show a men's team as well, to end our ROF series of photographs, also taken in the early 1980s. Some of the team are; B. Quinn, A. Rothwell, Les Clark, E. Aspey and Dave Brewer.

These images of ROF Chorley in the 1970s and early '80s, I hope will show that it was more than just a place to work at. It was a community in its own right.

This photograph dates from the early 1970s and shows Chorley Parish Church and Market Street/Union Street corner without traffic lights. Notice the mill chimneys, the Parish Institute, houses in Water Street, and the shadow of the Town Hall clock tower to the lower right.

ND - #0223 - 270225 - C0 - 246/189/9 - PB - 9781780914893 - Gloss Lamination